THE EFFICIENTPRENEUR

A Practical Guide to Transition from
Employee to Efficient Entrepreneur

By Ahmed Al Kiremli

Author Contact: ahmedalkiremli.com

AK Publishing LLC
616 Corporate Way, Suite 2-4718
Valley Cottage, NY 10989

Library of Congress Control Number: 2017947927

ISBN: 978-0-9993576-9-9

First Printing: 2017

This book has provided the most accurate information possible. Many of the techniques used in this book are from personal experiences. The author shall not be held liable for any damages resulting from use of this book.

DEDICATION

This book is dedicated to entrepreneurs—and those who would like to be—fighting to make their dreams a reality. Without your sacrifice, mankind would not enjoy the quality of life and innovation that you have brought us. Thank you for making your mark on this world through your products, services, inventions and achievements. You have shaped the future.

TABLE OF CONTENTS

INTRODUCTION

"The best time to plant a tree was 20 years ago.
The second-best time is now."
— Chinese proverb

The number one struggle for most people around the world today is money. But, surprisingly, the cause of widespread financial hardship is not a lack of cash—after all, there's an abundance of money circulating in the world today.

Instead, the main source of personal financial hardship is more often a lack of financial education—that is, not knowing even how to acquire the right financial knowledge.

In this book, I'll reveal the reasons why this lack of knowledge exists and discuss what you need to do to prevent the financial struggle in future. More importantly, I want to help you eliminate the struggle—and become financially free—by transitioning from employee to efficient entrepreneur, with the least amount of risk possible.

I coined the term *Efficientpreneur* because I have met many entrepreneurs who are stressed out and working long hours, just as unhappy as in the days when they were employees. Efficientpreneurship is a combination between two words Efficiency and Entrepreneurship. Becoming an entrepreneur is an important first step, but just the first step. To truly enjoy the freedom of time and money that entrepreneurship offers, you must become efficient and wise in the way you use your time and energy.

Through the pages of this book, you'll be armed with the knowledge you need to move form employment to entrepreneurship. And if you've already made the move, you'll discover how to more efficiently run your business by becoming an Efficientpreneur so you can cut the hours you spend and more easily achieve the outcomes you want. Together, we'll design an efficient plan to run your business with the maximum performance possible—and without losing your life.

The Progression of Mankind Through Four Economic Stages

The world as we know it today is the product of constant economic growth and progression since the dawn of mankind. But looking back, we can see four distinct "economic ages" in which people earned income or survived differently. Starting with the Hunter-Gatherer Age—where humans relied on nature to provide wealth via hunting animals and gathering plants—people lived in tribal groupings for security. During this Age, all people were poor—living at basically the same financial level. If you didn't know how to hunt and gather effectively, you died.

During the Agrarian Age, land became the most valuable asset. Land owners became rich from their lands, while peasants who worked the land were generally poor. Later, the Industrial Age dawned with the onset of the Industrial Revolution—widely regarded as a transition to new manufacturing processes from 1760 to about 1840. During the Industrial Age, the value of land was judged not by its ability to grow crops, but rather by its ability to provide the raw materials needed for manufacture—hematite ore for producing iron, coal for running machinery, gas for lighting cities, copper, tin, rubber, oil and other resources to help industry grow. Millions of workers relied on jobs for their income, ushering in a "middle class" of people who were neither upper-class asset owners nor surviving in poverty at the whim of crops and weather.

For more than 150 years, the Industrial Age built modern countries, economies, companies and consumers. But in 1989, as the Berlin Wall fell and the Cold War began to thaw, the dawn of the Information Age accelerated this development. The gap between rich and poor widened to create a new class—the super-rich—while the middle class began to struggle and, some authorities say, began to disappear altogether.

During each of these four great economic ages, the rules of money—and how money was earned—evolved. In the Agrarian and Industrial Age, for instance, ordinary people earned what became known as "active" or "linear" income by working for other people (either land owners or factory owners). They exchanged their time for money. Portfolio income also came into being as asset owners began to buy and sell real estate for capital gain or trade for different types of products.

Passive income, established during the Agrarian Age, meant that landowners could earn continuous cash-flow through renting their land to tenant farmers. In this Industrial Age, passive income was also earned, but through the ownership of businesses, factories and industrial resources. But in the Information Age, passive income became more pronounced as it skyrocketed many young people into the super-rich class by technology, the automation of processes, and the lightning-fast movement of information.

In this book, we'll examine these different types of income and learn where you should focus to become financially free. Whether you choose to earn income through business, real estate, paper assets, or commodities, I will show you clear examples of how you should invest to earn money—without sacrificing your life, without working only for money, and without ignoring the people you love or the things that make you feel fulfilled.

Depend on Yourself, Not Government

Most governments are struggling financially. Some are even going bankrupt because of embedded entitlements such as social security, healthcare and pensions. Over the years, each created massive bills for these governments to pay—and the debts they've created are increasing without solution. Unfortunately, the problem is even more acute, since these same governments have taught their people to depend on government instead of relying on themselves.

As of May 2016, the United States debt was over $19 TRILLION dollars. More than half of this debt obligation is due to America's social security, pension and healthcare costs. And it's increasing year after year because people have learned (wrongly) to depend on government. They've been poisoned through an education system based on old ideas. And government continues to apply strategies that worked during the Industrial Age, while we actually exist in the Information Age. Government is creating a nation of spenders rather than producers—a nation that doesn't know the difference between an asset and a liability, or how to invest. Instead, they know how to max out their credit cards. Even more of a game-changer, the life expectancy of humans is increasing thanks to technology and modern medicine—with workers living 20-50 years beyond their retirement date—resulting in even bigger social security, pension obligations and healthcare costs for government.

Entrepreneurial Knowledge Is Power

We are in the Information Age. Most people believe they need to acquire as much information as they can consume. But the problem with the increase in information through different platforms is that it all becomes "noise." People are more confused than ever about what to follow. What we need in not information but *knowledge*. We need imagination to pursue our goals and dreams more efficiently.

This book will focus on this objective.

Of course, while *information* is important, it's not as valuable as *knowledge*. Knowledge gives you the ability to filter out unimportant information, as well as the power to act upon what is essential. For example, oil is valuable, but by itself it doesn't make you rich. *Understanding* how it can be used to create wealth is what will make you rich.

Entrepreneurship—the understanding of how to use the resources available to you to create wealth—is your high-speed ticket to financial freedom. Of course, it is not an easy or risk-free path. Unlike employment—a job which requires specialized knowledge about very few things—entrepreneurship requires learning a little about many different things. While risky in the short-term, it's safer than employment which is only a short-term solution to lifelong financial struggle. Employment also creates stress, not just in existing from paycheck to paycheck, but because one's knowledge becomes so specialized that losing a job is truly a crisis.

When you fail in business, on the other hand, you learn to adjust, taking wiser, more focused action the next time you pursue a goal. If you fail at one aspect of business, your generalized knowledge allows you to float—doing something that buys you time until you find a way to make your business model work. In many ways, the world of business demands that entrepreneurs learn something new every day. Just learning everything you need to learn to run a business is a substantial education. So, don't let the potential of failure in business and in life overshadow the excitement of winning. Life will push you around. Do your best. Start small, think big. Leverage what others have learned in the areas where you want to succeed. Never settle or quit until you achieve your dream.

You and I Are Similar When It Comes to Life Experience

If you are seriously considering pursuing entrepreneurship, but hesitate to leave the "security" of employment, realize that I feel your pain. I've been there, too. I've lived the pain of running out of money while still having to uphold family financial responsibilities. I've lived both the pain of having to pay bills on time and the shame of bouncing checks. I've had to wake up early in the morning to arrive on time to a job that I don't like. And I've spent many sleepless nights as I pursued my financial goals.

I believe I know other types of pain you've been faced with, too. Perhaps it's the let-down of a mutual fund company whom you trusted with your savings and retirement money. Or the pain of credit card debt. The pain of a fixed income that didn't grow for years—while your expenses seemed to increase by leaps and bounds. I understand the lack of control over your life and worrying about your children's future. I've experienced the pain of the bad economy—wasting money because of the mistakes of government bureaucrats. In the past, I too experienced times in my life when I had very little time (even no time) to spend with family and the people I love. I've lived with the nonsense of a difficult boss. I've lived the pain of tolerating office politics and enduring workplace standard that don't make any sense. I feel your pain because I've been there.

But running away from the problem isn't going to solve it—whether you're still an employee or have since started your own business. As with any hurdle, the solution will only come with practice. Yes! Practice.

You'll find that entrepreneurship is like a sport: you need to struggle, hustle and show up every day to achieve impressive results. You need to plan, start, fail at different things, admit your failure, learn from it, stand on your feet again, adjust what went wrong—then start again with a better plan and better execution.

Fulfillment and Wealth Are Two Different Things

While you're pursuing financial freedom, remember that many wealthy people are rich in monetary terms but, in their mind, *they are poor*. They're chasing a number that's constantly going up—and the chase consumes their entire life. That's not a fulfilling, compelling, exciting life. And it's one reason why this book is not just about making money, but about lifestyle freedom and lasting fulfillment, too.

Financial freedom means working because *you want to*, not because (financially) you have to. It means you get to choose when you take a break—whether it's day off, a two-week vacation or a month-long sabbatical. Not only are you both "on break" and "at work" all the time—you get to juggle both in any way you like, so you can enjoy both your breaks and your work life as you see fit.

Financial freedom puts you in the driver's seat.

Unfortunately for most people, staying in control—being in the driver's seat—requires strategic planning and focused action, all of which comes at a price. But most people are not willing to pay that price. This unwillingness is made worse by the fact that the prevailing "wisdom" passed on to young people is to go to school, get good grades, land a high-paying job—then diversify by putting your money into mutual funds so you can retire at age 65 and let the government take care of you. With this kind of childhood programming, is it any wonder that most people play it safe in the short term, yet as a result, stay limited their entire lives? They're not willing to pay the price and do those things that will lead them to financial freedom. In fact, most people are still operating under Industrial Age career planning, when the Information Age has changed all the rules.

This book, on the other hand, is your guidebook to the new rules. You'll learn to start and manage a business that you can leverage through a team or a system. You'll learn to take control to improve your life and secure your future. The goal is *not* to own a business that *requires more hours of work than your current job*. With the systems you'll learn to develop, you'll have a business that works without you most of the time.

These are the same systems—the same efficient and strategic way of running a business—that have allowed me to create several companies in different industries. I designed them to run using a certain system, then I delegate the management and operations to my team or sign with franchisees or business partners, which allows me to relax from the management after building and testing a system I can trust. I try to eliminate myself from operations as much as possible in order to create more time for myself to innovate new ways to support my teams or businesses—enabling them to prosper and expand even more.

With this approach, I usually have more time to spend with people I love, such as family and friends, and to discover the world and enjoy life. The most precious thing for me is having the amount of freedom that I want and time to learn more from books, seminars, webinars, blogs and mentors. This is where I spend most of my time: learning all I can in order to add value to my businesses and leave the world a better place. This is what creates fulfillment in my life.

As an entrepreneur in transition from employment, this book will help you run your business more efficiently and achieve bigger results with less time, less effort and lower costs.

In Closing: One Final, Unique Reason Why I Chose Entrepreneurship Over Employment. What's Your Unstoppable Goal?

Before you turn the page to begin your own journey as an entrepreneur, I'd like to share a story from my life that illustrates how, aside from the financial freedom I was seeking, making the choice to become an entrepreneur changed my circumstances in an unusual and delightful way—as I believe it will change yours.

If you would have asked me a year ago, what I'd regret if I died tomorrow, I would have said that it was missing my chance to play squash in the world professional tour. As a young person, I was on the Iraqi National team for over 10 years—playing the fast-paced racket sport on indoor courts all over the country. I was even ranked number one in Iraq for 7 years straight. But living in Iraq—a closed country during the 1990s with a local sports federation that was riddled with corruption—made the dream of playing on the world tour literally impossible, even if my finances could afford it (which they couldn't).

In 2005, I moved to Dubai—continuing to play squash on an amateur level when I had extra time. In my heart, however, I knew my dream was on hold indefinitely, since I could never take the time off work to travel the world for professional competitions as I had once wanted so badly. Soon, with the pressure of work life, I also started gaining weight. And eventually, my weight gain triggered gout disease—something my father had suffered for years. Playing soccer one evening with some friends, I damaged my ACL—ultimately choosing to have surgery a year later. With a knee injury, gout-ridden feet and an office job that never seemed to provide enough time for practice, it seemed my dream of playing squash professionally was something I would never be able to do.

Entrepreneurship changed all that. But most importantly, it changed my outlook.

Today, I travel the world competing in the Professional Squash Association World Ranking Tour. Starting in February 2016, I managed to drop my weight and play with my restructured ACL knee—a challenge at my age of 35. I began with a world ranking of 422 and thought, *Let's do it just to feel good and say that I have done it. What do I have to lose? At least I'll have traveled the world and discovered new places.*

Within six months, I had reached a new world rank of 293. By January 2017 I hit a new record world ranking of 273 and visited more than 15 countries in less than 12 months. Meeting all these new people and seeing new places taught me much and expanded my business opportunities.

How was I able to accomplish all this when I thought my professional sports career was over?

Because I jumped in and took action—and because I've since achieved financial freedom—all these elements contributed to this accomplishment. It's a priceless experience and a journey that I was almost doomed to regret forever.

You, too, deserve to live your life to the highest level of fulfillment. When you do, you'll not only achieve your dreams, you'll leave a legacy for other to follow. I'll do my very best to guide you through the process in the following chapters.

To aid you in understanding and implementing the information in this book, I've created a special gift for you. Please visit ahmedalkiremli.com/book to claim it.

CHAPTER 1

EMPLOYEE OR ENTREPRENEUR?

"Whenever culture has gone through a radical change, as ours has—
from industrial age to information age — there are people who will deny that
things have changed; they resist it and refuse to change."
— Daniel Greenberg

An employee is an individual who works part-time or full-time for another individual or enterprise, by verbal or written agreement or contract, for financial benefit or other compensation. The word "entrepreneur" first appeared in the French dictionary in 1723 as someone who starts and runs a small business or multiple businesses, becomes responsible for all risks and rewards of a given business venture, and is commonly seen as a leader and innovator of new ideas and business processes. At some point in your life, maybe right now, you will want to determine which of these ways of earning income is the best vehicle for your success and financial freedom.

Many people think that the era of the employee has been around forever, that 99% of people are employees and the rest are entrepreneurs. But if you read about the Agrarian Age, you discover that most people were entrepreneurs — mainly self-employed entrepreneurs and a few business owners.

You can figure that out from most of the people, whose last names used to refer to the professions people mastered during that age, such as Baker, Potter and Taylor. Later, when the Industrial Age arrived and throughout the 18th, 19th and early 20th centuries, the demand for employees increased and the entire system changed. More benefits for employees were developed, so most workers were secured for life by pension plans that were created at the time. In 1920, a mandatory requirement with a small company pension evolved to move older workers aside. In the 1920s, most railroad workers were covered by pensions. In the U.S., the Employment Retirement Income Security Act of 1974 (ERISA) increased pension funding requirements.

In 1971, American President Richard Nixon removed the United States dollar from the gold standard—permanently ending the Bretton Woods system of international financial exchange whose ideas had been shaped in 1944. This single action ushered in an era of freely floating currencies that remains in effect to this day. Nixon's decision in 1971 is continually debated to be one of the main causes for the 2007-2008 financial crisis.

The Industrial Age became a golden era for employees and then changed again for them when the Information Age emerged after the fall of the Berlin Wall. In the Information Age, machines began to replace employees. The number of college graduates increased but many of them struggled to find a job. The pension system changed, decreasing employee security. The Information Age provided employees with higher risk but, at the same time, opened a whole new era of opportunities thanks to the Internet.

In the Information Age, the Internet and outsourcing model had a global effect. One of the important books that discusses this era of change is *The World Is Flat.*[1] In this book author Thomas L. Friedman discusses how the invention of fiber optic cables played a significant role in transferring information that connects the world in a faster way. These cables help demolish perceived vertical walls between countries and expanded a horizontal exchange of information in the world, enhancing humanity globally by sharing and interchanging ideas, products, knowledge and experience.

Four Basic Ways People Earn Income

In the book, *The Cashflow Quadrant,* Robert Kiyosaki[2] developed a genius conceptual diagram to categorize the four major ways income is earned, calling it the cashflow quadrant. It consists of two crossed lines (one vertical, one horizontal) shaping the + sign. The word "employee" appears in the top left corner of the diagram, "self-employed" in the lower left corner, "business owner" in the top right corner, and "investor" on the lower right.

Capital letters are used to further illustrate each of the four quadrants. For example, "E" stands for an employee who works for somebody else in exchange for money or other benefits, based on a contractual arrangement or agreement, and who works within a certain timeframe to perform certain tasks and authorities. Most people in the employee quadrant work to generate income.

"S" stands for such self-employed or specialists as dentists, doctors, mechanics, carpenters, or small business owners who have created jobs for themselves or created a business they own that they must physically be on-site to manage. Most of the time they work longer hours than the typical employee and certainly longer than the hours they worked when they were employees.

---

[1] Friedman, Thomas L. *The World Is Flat: A Brief History of the Twenty-first Century.* NY: Farrar, Straus and Giroux, 2005. This will stay as reference?

[2] Kiyosaki, Robert T. with Sharon L. Lechter, C.P.A. *Rich Dad's Cashflow Quadrant: Rich Dad's Guide to Financial Freedom.* NY: Grand Centeral Publishing, 2001

"B" stands for those who own a business that generates a passive income but who don't have to physically be there to run the business. These are people who own a system that generates money automatically without their physical involvement. In this quarter, you find more financially free, wealthy people. Business owners generate portfolio (capital gains income) or passive income (cash flow income).

"I" represents the investor, who uses money to create more money by investing in a variety of assets such as businesses, real estate, paper assets and commodities. For investors, money works for them instead of them working for the money. Investors generate portfolio (capital gains income) or passive income (cash flow income).

The goal is to shift from the left side of the quadrant (E and S) — because on this side it's difficult to acquire long-term wealth — to the right side of the quadrant (B and I) where you can be financially free, wealthy, working for portfolio and cash flow income. As a side note, working for cash flow income is more important than working for portfolio income, but the more innovative you get as a business owner or investor, the better you become at generating both types of income by using your own source of skills to create your own successful formula of income generation.

Advantages of Being an Employee

"When you are young, work to learn, not to earn."
—Robert Kiyosaki

Fixed Income

Receiving a fixed and steady income at the end of each month is one of the major benefits of being an employee. You know exactly how much you're going to make and you can plan your expenses accordingly. Having a known fixed income will give you peace of mind, in the short run.

Fixed Working Hours

Employees work generally from 9 am to 5 pm, maybe longer hours or shorter hours. Whether full-time or part-time, they know how long they are supposed to work. Many stay longer to demonstrate their value, to get a promotion or a raise. Some are more motivated as employees because they focus on a certain targeted track; they often work 15% to 30% longer hours because that's their way of showing productivity in their lives in terms of work. Productivity is a great source of happiness and self-satisfaction.

Less Responsibility

Employees get orders from their employers and don't need to think as much about what they are doing. They follow orders and tend to focus on one targeted area, which they hopefully keep improving. Some employees are not concerned about a decision going wrong because the blame will rest on whoever gave them the order to implement the decision. Some employees sometimes buy time just to get their salary at the end of the month, with less and less duty and pressure from their managers, often wasting time in implementing some tasks or projects. This is why continuous tracking and follow-up on employees is important.

Less Risk in the Short Term

Most employees live check to check. In the short term, there's less risk. Down the road, in the long-term, there's more risk, because the older you get, the greater your expenses with such pressures in life as marriage, kids, schools and universities for your children, medical bills, day-to-day living expenses, and perhaps a better lifestyle you'd like to live. But when you begin, there's not much risk at all.

Even when you move to another job with a higher salary, your expenses tend to go up because you either lack investing skills or are likely to feel an inner desire to achieve a higher standard of living to match your new salary.

Also, because employees structure their mindset and life around a job, you may keep yourself busy looking for one job after another. If you are out of a job, you'll feel the pressure, especially if you aren't prepared to get involved in a different kind of opportunity. When opportunity knocks, there's usually not enough time to think wisely and take the best action.

As an employee, you are focused on one area only to which you devote complete effort. If the company for which you work goes bankrupt, you're not the one responsible. Even if you're the CEO, as an employee you can't be sued for the bankruptcy of your employer. It's different from being an entrepreneur, when you take full responsibility for everything legal and beyond — especially if you don't know how to protect yourself when you sign with your investors, partners, suppliers, customers or any other second or third party.

The Challenges Tend to Be Known

As an employee, your experience is based on years of specific skills you've learned from companies for which you've worked, so usually you know the challenges you're going to face. Perhaps you'll face tougher targets or greater challenges when you achieve more and get promoted; but in most cases, you'll continue to work in the same area in which you excel, except maybe in the first few years of your career as an employee maybe you will test different companies, industries or departments until you focus on a specific industry or department.

In most cases, an employee usually knows lots of technical details about one subject matter. When airline pilots lose their jobs at age 50 or older, they panic because they've trained all their lives to do one thing, fly a plane.

Development and Growth Are Key

Graduating college students often head straight to a multinational company to learn about its system and environment. Becoming an employee with such a company at the beginning of your career is the best thing to do — to focus on learning its system if you are hoping to do something similar in the future.

What matters most is how much you're going to learn. Working for such a company provides you with free training, skill development and experience.

As a young employee, I jumped from job to job looking only at the numbers, how much they would pay me. My target was to jump from a certain number to a higher number, regardless of any other factors involved in signing a contract. With experience, when considering a new job, I realized that I was starting to think about more in-depth matters: Salary is important, but who will be my manager? What's the environment I'm going to work in? Will I be learning something new? Will there be excellent training? What kind of company am I working for in terms of industry and size, and what's my future with this company in the long run?

Different Extra Benefits

In certain countries, employees get free healthcare for themselves and their families, get retirement benefits, have a fixed paid leave for 15 to 30 days a year, plus sick leave. Employees will naturally feel more secure when they have a job with these kinds of benefits.

When people lose their jobs, sometimes the only path they know is to look for another job, because they believe that it's the only safe path for them in the world. They shift from one employment confinement to another. While their goal is to seek security, in my opinion they take the biggest risk in their lives by pursuing careers as employees — continuing to jump from one job to another, dreaming of becoming rich by following this model, while continuing to work for ordinary earned income.

Disadvantages of Being an Employee

"The bravest sight in the world is to see
a great man struggling against adversity."
— Seneca

Waking Up Early

I'm not a morning person. For me it was always difficult to wake up early in the morning; however, most of my career has been in sales. A company cares more about numbers than time, so that's what I used to focus on to make up for my late mornings.

Everyone has his or her time to be most productive. Always try to find yours. For me, it's usually late at night because there is less noise and fewer distractions. It's tiring sometimes to work late and wake up late. I suffer from insomnia and often cannot switch off my brain but I'm working on solving this issue over time. Fortunately, I manage all my current businesses wirelessly even though most of them are offline businesses; but I still manage them online. So I can be my most productive during my best hours, and achieve my tasks and goals.

Urgency and Routine

Life is full of urgency – waking up early in the morning, shutting off noisy alarm clocks, quickly eating breakfast, getting your children to school, or dropping your spouse somewhere. All of this is perhaps achieved before you get to work at 9 a.m.

After reaching your office you urgently have your coffee to jump quickly into emails which are checked 20 times a day, via your computer and/or your smart phone; then you finish the day with quick meetings, quickly dash back home, get stuck in the traffic, reach home exhausted, have a quick dinner with your family — your kids if they are still awake — then you wait for the weekend to sleep for one full day and get drunk the second day or just spend it with the family somewhere. Does this sound familiar? It's a common pattern for many people.

Often we see posts on Facebook: "Yay, the weekend is here!" "Yay, today is a public holiday, I wish all days were holidays!" This is the life of employees. Even their vacations are all about urgency — some trying to visit a country in three days and get to know it in that time.

Lack of Control and Authority

As an employee, you are limited and attached to a job, and you have no authority or control over decisions, depending on your job description and level; in most cases, even high-level positions still have certain limitations.

Risk of Losing a Job

As an employee, you are always under the threat of being laid off. There's no guarantee that you'll stay with the company forever. In years past, employees would work for companies all their lives; not so today. There are many variables these days in any company. Some companies tend to keep their employees longer than others. If you want to secure longer employment, you always must be in the lead and make the company feel that it would be a huge loss for them if they lost you.

Regardless of how hard you work to secure your job, many things can change. Sometimes top management evolves, or the company goes through a merger or joint venture. Your manager may be fired and the new one wants to bring in his or her own new team. Many new managers opt to change anything to show their superiors that they are changing something for the better, regardless of whether it's right or wrong.

Some people shift from being an employee to being a business owner, but still get trapped by creating a job they can never leave. This is better than being an employee — at least they have more control over their situation, more authority, more decisions to change their reality — but, as we've mentioned, they will likely work longer hours than they worked as an employee. New business-owners can lose interest in developing into entrepreneurs because owning one's own business is challenging — making all the decisions, motivating themselves as well as their employees.

For those who are self-employed, the great disadvantage is that when they stop working, the money stops. Many of them believe that to "do the job right" they need to do it themselves; they operate under the one-man-show business model. As a result, they often continue struggling all their lives, limited in terms of freedom and money. They are usually perfectionists who don't like to delegate, and like to do things their own way because they believe they are the only people in the world who can do the things the way they do — but you know better. Some types of employees are rich, especially doctors and dentists, but most of them have limited income because employees usually work for ordinary earned income and when they stop working for any reason, the money stops.

Fear and Struggles After Losing Your Job

After you are laid off, life shuts down, you feel bad and you start looking through newspaper ads, job websites and sending your résumé everywhere. This results in your going on interviews. If the economy is bad, there's the uncertainty of not being able to find a job within a month, or even a year — or longer.

It's normal for employees to go through this process, but why? Why not become an entrepreneur and start your own business? People sometimes spend 40 years learning how to do and keep the right job. Others break through as entrepreneurs in a year or two from a small online or offline startup project.

I'm not saying that you should quit your job, but you must always learn. Keep learning and start focusing on other options. Your job or your career is not the only option available to you. There is high risk in the long term of being an employee; the older you get, the more difficult it is to get another job doing the same thing.

Work Politics and Policies

At any company, big or small, there are always company politics, whether you like them or not. Right or wrong, you have to follow them. You may experience unfair decisions or see wrong policies that take time to get improved or even changed; some never get changed. You will see that some managers are more flexible with employees and/or that some employees are paid more than they deserve, or that some money is spent on things you perceive as unwise — all for reasons that no one can understand, and no one is willing to explain.

Limited Income

As an employee, you help your employer get richer while you still have limited income that changes every couple of years — rarely enough to handle your expenses, feed your dreams, or deal with the rate of inflation.

Why stay limited? Why don't you use your time to learn and master some new skills so you can build your own business, hire your own employees, become rich or, at least, financially free?

Limited Time

As we've already discussed, even if you're a CEO of a company, you'll still be attached to a job for which you have some flexibility but also more responsibility. You push yourself more, exhaust yourself by adding more hours to your day to keep up with the competition and because you need to keep the CEO chair, and because your financial responsibility, lifestyle and dreams have grown. At the same time, you have less time with your family, which creates more stress.

Limited Mobility

Because you're forced to earn money, you may have to live in a place you don't really like much or don't like at all. I have seen friends working in the oil and gas sector, living in horrible places for months, sometimes in caravans far offshore in the middle of the sea, far from their families and the rest of the world.

With limited time to travel the way you want, and always rushing because you are between resting and enjoying your vacation, you may not even enjoy that time. Not every vacation provides the kind of relaxation you may need, especially if you are travelling with family.

At one point in my life, I decided to move from a high-paying job to one that paid 40% less than my previous salary. At that stage of my life, my existence was less about money and more about my environment, how happy I would be, how comfortable it would be to work in those surroundings, and how much I would learn. This I credit as a factor in my beginning to think and take steps to become an entrepreneur.

Advantages of Becoming an Entrepreneur

An entrepreneur tends to bite off a little more than
he can chew hoping he'll quickly learn how to chew it."
— Roy Ash

Some companies today are working toward making their work environment more entrepreneurial so their employees can think outside the box of the company's usual way of solving problems. This is healthy for the company atmosphere and its customers, but if you're an employee in this situation, as long as you continue to receive a fixed paycheck, you're still an employee. That's why it's best to not fool yourself into thinking that, if your company's approach is entrepreneurial, you are an entrepreneur. The best course to take in this situation is to learn from your environment — acquire some good skills and prepare for your next challenge of developing into a real entrepreneur.

Becoming an entrepreneur is a process that takes time, so it's important to not rush it. Learn all you can and open yourself to enjoy the process of becoming more knowledgeable. You may face some tough times on the way, but you'll also confront opportunities that could open new doors.

Any entrepreneur can come from an employment background, having acquired skills and experience that help movement to the next level and then on to full entrepreneurship. But the question is: In which quarter of the cashflow quadrant does the entrepreneur operate? The answer: Usually as a self-employed business owner or investor. For example, the small shop business owner is an entrepreneur but still a self-employed person. The business owner who owns a business that's operated as a system is an entrepreneur who owns and manages a company without getting involved in company operations so the business can run on autopilot most of the time.

The entrepreneur mainly operates as S or B but sometimes gets into investment deals — whether as a bootstrapper, by investing personal resources in his or her own business, or as an angel investor by investing in other businesses. One can invest in real estate, paper assets or commodities along with ownership of a business.

The advantages of entrepreneurship are many. Here are a few that are the most important for me.

Freedom: Time for What You Enjoy

One of the primary advantages of being an entrepreneur is having freedom — the freedom of time, to spend time with family and/or friends. I think time is the most precious thing in life, more important than money, which is why enjoying or spending your time the way you prefer is the greatest advantage you have as an Efficientpreneur.

Many entrepreneurs think that the primary goal in life is to make money. It's an important goal but not the main one; what's important is to live a happy and fulfilled life. Time allows you to create money if you are using your time and skills wisely. Money will not give you more years to live. Money can't give you extra time in your life. But it can save you time to leverage the power to be more efficient in whatever you want to achieve.

Apart from earning money, by using time wisely, you can create the greatest impact by adding value to other people's lives, so when you die you leave this world a better place.

By being an Efficientpreneur. you earn the freedom to:

- Follow your purpose and practice your passion.
- Work from wherever you want, any time you want.
- Live in the country of your choice for as long as you like.
- Wake up and go to sleep any time you wish.
- Play any sport you like anytime you wish.
- Enjoy your time with family and friends.

As a traditional entrepreneur, you may make more money by exhausting yourself trying to do everything on your own, but it will leave you no time for a personal life, because you'll work longer hours than you worked as an employee. You will shift from the employment rat race to the traditional entrepreneur rat race, which will not help you live the happy life you want to live. Your freedom of choice will not be what you intend.

In Control of Your Path

As an entrepreneur, you will be able to make most of your own decisions. You'll make some mistakes, but you'll learn from them, so with time and practice you'll become more confident in yourself and more in control of your path, which will result in a better future. As an entrepreneur, the decision and control joystick is in your hand. Having that kind of control is a remarkably great feeling and will allow you to turn the impossible into possible if you know how to dream big and take consistent action to make your dreams a reality.

Acquiring Authority and Recognition

An entrepreneur is a leader rather than a follower. This station puts you in a position of earning recognition from other people, appearing unique because you are the inventor, founder and creator of whatever you are creating — perhaps a project or company, or maybe a movement to save people in Africa. Being a follower is not a bad thing — we are all followers at one time or another — we need to learn to be good followers to become good leaders. But leaders have a greater impact on people and on the world. Now is your time to build better ideas, provide more value to others, and inspire everyone around you. When employees invent something while employed, the invention is most often registered under the company name by law.

Sometimes the name of the inventor employee is mentioned, and sometimes not.

Building a Stronger Network

Networking with more people at different levels is another advantage of entrepreneurship. You will meet many other people from different companies, and likely network inside and outside your company; how often and how much depends on the size and quality of your network, the events you attend, and the companies you target. Some employees have larger networks than entrepreneurs, but in general and with the nature of the entrepreneurial life, entrepreneurs not only have a more expansive network than employees, but they tend to network at a higher and more targeted level, using such connections to open many doors for future business deals, partnerships, financing for projects and different investment opportunities.

Adding Value Through Innovation

When you are in the process of inventing a new product or new service to make other people's lives easier, or help solve a problem, what you must think about is how to add value to other people's lives. Helping others by adding value will make you successful. When you add value, the money will follow.

Laying the Path to Independence

Being an entrepreneur gives you independence — it gives you the confidence to make your own decisions and to be in control of your own path as it is shaped by your own decisions.

Growing Your Limitless Income

As an employee, you're limited regardless of how much you make, even if it's $1 million a year. You are still limited to $1 million with limited growth over time due to the lack of leverage, and this million might disappear anytime if you lose your job. Most employees spend most of what they make and don't know how to invest the remainder. The more their income climbs, the more their expenses rise. Also, your life as an employee is most often centered on jumping from one job to another every certain number of years.

As an entrepreneur, you're able to reach a limitless state of income based on your actions, skills, innovation and mindset. There are usually no limits for income if you know what you're doing. You may jump from one project to another, while the previous project is still working and growing, adding value to others, and earning more income for you.

I have been offered many jobs during my entrepreneurial life that earn me five to ten times more than what I'm making as an entrepreneur. At first, it was difficult to resist the offers — sometimes I went to the interviews, but over time I programmed my mind to say that regardless of the job or the size of the check at the end of the month, I would not accept it. That was because my thinking had already begun to shift from a short-term, narrow-thinking employee to a wide, long-term thinking, Efficientpreneur. An employee thinks of the fat paycheck at the end of the month; an entrepreneur thinks of a possible small check at first but in time this check will grow in value based on the automation, leverage and system you use.

As an example, I might make $3,000 per month as an entrepreneur and get an offer of $12,000 per month as an employee. I would turn down the $12,000 offer because I know that by sticking to my entrepreneurial position and continuing to learn and improve my skills, I will make $100,000 per month after a few years. It's a whole other mindset.

Sizing Up Your Tax Benefits

An entrepreneur has superior tax benefits in most countries of the world. There are a few countries that have no taxes, but most do. An entrepreneur or business is most often taxed at a lower rate than that of an employee who works in a country with tax laws.

Appreciating the Flexibility of Choosing Your Own Team

As an entrepreneur, you can hire whatever team you wish, select and work with the people you choose, and fire the people you don't want. You can live wherever you want, and travel wherever you want to go, anytime you wish and let your team grow your company for you if the system that you have designed is efficient enough.

Living with the Excitement of Change

Entrepreneurs experience more adventure and consistent change throughout their projects or businesses. The risks are always there when you start, but become less the more you practice the game and get to know the rules. Change is exciting, and it's important to enjoy it. Excitement comes also from the flexibility of making decisions as well as the generation involved in a new product or service created from scratch and becoming top-of-the-line. It's exciting to build a brand from scratch, to think about how to market it as well as the look of its logo.

You know how you sometimes participate in a sport with others and suffer through the game, but after you play the game and finish your shower, you feel a special feeling of excitement, comfort and relief at the same time? The excitement of being an entrepreneur has that same kind of unique feeling that you'll never understand until you live it.

Disadvantages of Becoming an Entrepreneur

"A pessimist sees the difficulty in every opportunity;
an optimist sees the opportunity in every difficulty."
—Winston Churchill

The Challenge of Responsibility

If you are not willing to be responsible, entrepreneurship is not for you — stay away from it and maintain your peace of mind. As a business owner, you need to be responsible for your decisions and for what's going on with the business. If you have financed or "bootstrapped" your own business, the pressure of responsibility might be lower; but when you're using other people's money (family and friends, angel investors, or venture capitalists), the game changes. Sometimes you're not responsible for everything but still might be blamed for everything, so you need to be prepared. If you're planning to be an entrepreneur one day, you need to learn how to be responsible for your mistakes and, most of the time, the mistakes of others.

Learning How to Handle Risk

An essential part of being a business owner is learning how to improve your risk management skills, so you can handle the risk of losing your money or investor money. You must learn how to protect yourself legally if something goes wrong with the business. It's important to understand what business entity to select when you establish your business, whether as a sole proprietorship, limited liability company

(LLC), C corporation (a corporation taxed separately from its owners) or S corporation (not taxed separately). You also need to ensure that the business contract between you and your partners, investors or franchisees is prepared by an attorney.

There are many balls to juggle to control risk and to protect your credibility. You must understand that your credibility is one of the most important assets as an entrepreneur, since investors have trusted you with their money and are investing in you because of your integrity. If you want to work with your partners or investors for the long term, which is how you must think, then you need to make sure that you take good care of them and keep your word so they trust you more over time. Trust in business is like marriage trust; it's the foundation of success.

Risk is necessary, but you must be careful calculating the risk you are getting into. If you're not taking action, you have zero probability of getting to the next level. If you take action through calculated risk, you'll have a higher probability of success; with time and more risks under your belt, your experience and knowledge will deliver a higher success rate.

The Art of Raising Capital

Raising capital — bootstrapping; tapping customers or family and friends; reaching out to banks, angel investors or venture capitalists — is one of the most difficult stages of entrepreneurship. It requires certain skills and puts anyone under a tremendous amount of pressure, especially in the early years of entrepreneurship.

Try as much as you can to stay away from financing your startup with family and friends unless they know how to deal with investments and financing. Most don't, and since you likely have a special emotional relationship with your family and friends, when money is involved, the relationship can be negatively affected. If you must involve them, be very careful so as not to lose them in the process. Be as clear as you can with them about the risk of your startup. Be detailed about your contract with them, mention clearly in the contract what's going to happen if the business makes money or loses money. Be especially clear with details that relate to losing money, because that's where problems most often arise. Finally, remember that contracts and explanations rarely cover every detail 100% perfectly. Time and experience will teach you what you need to know. All you can do is your best and hope for the best outcome.

Handling Disappointment

On your entrepreneurial journey, you'll face many crossroads, and be forced to make some quick, critical decisions in difficult times. Many of your decisions may trigger negative results, especially at the beginning, due to lack of experience and insufficient planning. It's essential to be prepared for big disappointments. Part of being an entrepreneur is about controlling your emotions during hard times so you can overcome the challenges you'll face down the road.

If the investment winds up losing, all fingers will point toward you. You'll be blamed for the outcome, and many people may make fun of you and underestimate you. Family and friends will tell you "We told you this wouldn't work." This is part of the usual drama of being an entrepreneur, so if you are not persistent enough to handle this kind of challenge, it's best to stay away from it and keep your job. But for me, this is what's exciting — this is how to learn.

Success is wonderful, but with success comes minimal learning. In life, failure is the best teacher.

Self-Doubt, Loneliness and Sleepless Nights

Welcome to the world of isolation, loneliness, not knowing what to do next, sleepless nights and loss of belief in yourself. These are common struggles of entrepreneurship. You have to deal with being alone with little or no support from others, and face sleepless nights thinking about how to solve a business disaster. You will live many years with the guilt of losing money of some investors. Many times, you'll find yourself sitting alone — in your flat, in the metro station, in a café — thinking about the next step, or the next project and ways to heal the pain from the previous failed venture or idea.

Family and friends who care about you might put you face-to-face with self-doubt because they want to give you their advice from a different perspective, based on their own life experiences, which often have little to do with yours. An example might be, say, that your father is an employee. He may never get what you're trying to do as an entrepreneur, because he's never attempted to be one. He may judge you, based on his experience, and while trying his best to protect you, his limited knowledge and experience won't be helpful. So, you need to believe your inner voice and choose mentors who've achieved what you want to achieve.

Sometimes we need to put all our money on the table before playing our cards. This is part of believing in one's self, listening to that inner voice and continuing to motivate yourself. Sometimes, I go to the cinema or play some sport to change my bad mood, and motivate myself to do what that inner voice is telling me to do.

**Always dig for the things that motivate you.
When you're feeling down, use them to
get back on the right track.**

Starting Is Tough

Starting is always difficult as a new entrepreneur. There are always struggles and disappointments, which are part of becoming a great entrepreneur. Steve Jobs, the co-founder of Apple, and Mark Zuckerberg, the founder of Facebook, both faced challenges when they started their companies. Most entrepreneurs fail more than once, and keep moving forward until they get it right. Some entrepreneurs succeed in one of their ventures and then fail badly, so they go bankrupt five or ten years later because something went wrong. Then they struggle a few years more because they lack the confidence, finance or skills to get into another business.

If you're going to fail, fail early and fast. It's best to do it in the beginning rather than when you're in your 50s, or later. When you're facing a venture that you realize has no hope for the success or the kind of growth you envision, you'll still have the time and energy to pursue another venture and seize other opportunities.

When you become an employer at the beginning of your life, you can develop skills and confidence in the process. Start small but think long-term and think big. Remember that at the start of your entrepreneurial life, you might double your working hours compared with your life as an employee. You'll have to think more creatively about many things at the same time and deal with a higher number of variables and challenges.

Sacrifices Are Part of the Picture

The entrepreneurship journey requires many sacrifices along the way at many stages; you must let go of lots of things — you need to forget about your comfort zone, having less leisure time and fewer fun activities, you'll need to replace some of your entertainment activity time with other activities that will add more value to your entrepreneurial journey, like reading a book about the startup world or networking with other entrepreneurs or investors. The harsh reality is that you are not only investing your money and might lose it all, but also, you're sacrificing quality time with your family and friends, especially at the beginning.

No Fixed Income Is a New Way of Life

Your entrepreneurial life will demand that you let go of the days of fixed and steady monthly income, and you'll need to expect some months with no income — maybe no income plus heavy expenses that will put you under tremendous pressure and heavy debt in certain cases. While this is a huge disadvantage, it's best to look at it from a different perspective. No fixed income now might result in unlimited income later, so always think positively. Even if you've done your proper homework, things can still go wrong regardless of how well you've prepared.

Learning Skills You Might Dislike

Let's say that you're an accountant, accustomed to sitting behind a desk in an office all your life studying, reading and calculating numbers. You're likely to struggle with learning the most important skills for being an entrepreneur like how to sell and to raise capital.

To improve your skills as a sales person, let's say that you want to convince your spouse to have dinner with you in a certain restaurant that you really like is not her or his favorite. This is a sales task, so you can use this skill in your life. Some people believe that sales people are evil human beings doing a job that's dishonest. In fact, not all sales people cheat or use misleading techniques; most are very clear, helpful and straight-forward. Selling is a must-learn skill for entrepreneurs.

At the beginning of your career as entrepreneur you are likely in charge of managing your business most of the time, unless you have a cofounder who's responsible for management. That's highly recommended if you are a technical person and like to focus on the technical side of the business.

Management is all about problem-solving and facing new challenges, so you need to be a good problem solver to overcome the issues you're bound to face internally and externally. Everybody complains about certain problems, but very few can solve them.

Heighten your personal value by becoming an efficient problem solver.

Solving problems begins with communicating well with your team, whether they are your employees, partners or investors.

Variables You'll Face

Sometimes there's a mystery regarding the variables you're likely to face as an entrepreneur. On your journey, many things will change along the way, such as the economy, competition and technology. Something could go wrong with your new location; perhaps the city is building a new road and it happens to block the front of your shop. Things go wrong all the time, but what's important is that, regardless of how trying the challenges are, you have the will to come back. When things are bad, you get stronger. You do that by rearranging things, putting yourself together to come back smarter and more aggressive, so that you can achieve your success.

Take the example of actor Sylvester Stallone. When he was a struggling actor, at some point he was so broke, he sold his wife's jewelry without telling her. At one point in his life, he ended up homeless. He wept when having to sell his dog for $25 in order to eat. Two weeks later, he saw a boxing match between Mohammed Ali and Chuck Wepner, which inspired him to write the well-known script *Rocky*. He got an offer for $125,000 for the script and turned it down because he wanted to star in the movie, but the studio wanted the leading role to go to someone who was a star. A few weeks later, the studio offered him twice that amount. He still refused.

Eventually, the studio said he could star in the movie but they'd give him only $35,000 for the script. The movie won an Academy Award for Best Picture, and Stallone was even nominated as Best Actor. The film was inducted into the American National Film Registry as one of the greatest movies ever made.

When Stallone got his $35,000, he returned to find his dog. The person who bought the dog refused to give him up. Stallone offered him $100, but the man refused. He offered $500, then $1,000. Stallone wound up paying him $15,000 and got his dog back.

Nowadays the more I learn, the more I walk through the fear of facing challenging variables. Your brain is the key to solving any problem, so make sure you invest in it heavily. Personally, I'm not yet rich but I'm financially free and I feel that I'm on the right path. Even if I lose everything and must start from zero again, I know that I can come back, and I know that I'm going to be wealthy and fulfilled. Being rich is not my first priority; all that matters to me is being financially free, happy and fulfilled.

In a nutshell, you must:

- Set a vision with large goals.
- Believe in your ability to overcome challenging variables.
- Create a plan and timeframe to execute your plan.
- Divide the large goals into smaller goals.
- Build your dream team and invest in people who can add value to your venture.
- Focus on what you love and what you are passionate about; delegate the rest.
- Create well-planned steps through consistent focused action, and stay away from shiny temptations that lack foundation.
- Review your achievements, assess your results; learn from your mistakes and the mistakes of others.
- Always aim to modify and re-start the process more intelligently and efficiently to achieve greater goals that will bring you fulfillment, happiness and financial freedom.

CHAPTER 2

MY PERSONAL
JOURNEY

"You can't connect the dots looking forward, you can only connect them looking backwards. So you have to trust that the dots will somehow connect in your future. You have to trust in something — your gut, destiny, life, karma, whatever. This approach has never let me down, and it has made all the difference in my life."
— Steve Jobs

We all grow up differently, in different environments with different parents or caretakers. I want to tell you a bit about my upbringing so you see how I arrived at the decisions I've made, as this might trigger thoughts of your own upbringing and how what you've learned might prove helpful to you.

My early learning days as an employee began when I was a child. I remember my father taking me with him to his stationery shop regularly. This is a practice done by most small business owners in Iraq and many other countries all over the world. Parents take their children with them so their children can develop a market sense and new skills while they are young. The market is a great teacher and the younger you experience it, the more easily you're able to get into it and understand it. In such markets you learn the simple and basic rules of trade, money collection, organizing a shop, retail and wholesale sales techniques, as well as communication with customers, and your shop team and other traders.

I remember learning a lot from conversations between my father and other traders or employees. We had a shop at the wholesale stationery market and a retail shop in a classy part of Baghdad. I got a different perspective from each shop since the wholesale environment is totally different from retail. At the time of this writing, my father still owns and operates these shops.

In the wholesale environment, I learned how to deal with suppliers, how to collect from and pay money to other traders we usually trade with, and how to buy and sell bulk quantities, as well as pack and deliver them to the traders that purchase from us. The atmosphere of the wholesale market always has a special feeling — nothing fancy or sophisticated, but a good place to learn. If you're a small entrepreneur and a parent, I advise you to take your child with you on occasion to share a sense of what you're doing.

In the retail shop, the environment was more organized and classy, but in a simple way — not like the well-known, branded shops. My father's stationery store was not, and to this day is not, "properly" branded, as he does not focus on certain brands or items. He often changes brands to provide the best quality and variety. Besides, there's no designated system to market a brand or position there. So, a customer who visits our shop experiences an adventure in exploring the range of our new items that we launch on an ongoing basis. Every new visit is likely to provide a frequent change in stationery choices, and sometimes also such items as toys and home supplies. I learned how to organize such items and place them on the shelves in an attractive way to make them more appealing to customers. I also learned how to handle money transactions, as well as how to market and sell products to our clients.

I was always eager to learn more and excel quickly at whatever I was doing in the shop. Things tended to develop at a slower pace than what I wanted to achieve. My father slowed me down and didn't know how to give me the support to excel at a different level. I never felt I had the right opportunity to grow and achieve what I wanted while I watched other employees enjoy better support and opportunities.

My father believed I was a loser, focused only on sports and entertainment. I can't deny that I was a spoiled kid, but I still knew that I had more to deliver but hadn't yet found the right playing field in which to excel.

I was continually off and on with my father's business because we would always argue. He and my uncle, his partner, never gave me the right opportunity or space to achieve what I wanted to deliver. I would start to work and then quit, work again and then quit. I would approach my father or he would approach me with another deal or structure of work, but our arrangements would never last. My father was interested in my learning, but mainly he wanted to use me as a member of his workforce to improve the business, and never taught in a well-structured manner. That was his ability as operator of a one-man-show business. He wanted to teach me how to be an employee under his guidance and help him improve his business — but not at a level to which I aspired.

My father and my uncle both lacked the proper vision to take the business to a new level, and also lacked knowledge of the best way to employ and train the right people to replace them in a structure that would help the business grow. Their business was managed in a very old-school way, and centered on their own way of doing things.

My Humble Beginnings as an Entrepreneur

I'm originally from Iraq and was born and raised in Baghdad, the capital city. If you're an employee in Iraq you're extremely poor, which was especially true during the 1990s and early 2000s. After the Gulf

War, Iraq suffered a devastating economic plunge. Also, there was no proper employment system in our corporate structure.

All Iraqi employees, whether they were working for the government or the private sector, had insignificant salaries. I know you will find it difficult to believe, but most public school teachers received from $3 to $10 per month. Doctors earned between $40 and $100 a month.

How did those people survive? They lived on a basic food supply distributed by the government on a monthly basis, or resorted to bribes or stealing or survived under very poor conditions. The country did not have much to spend on — no mobile telephone or satellite service allowed, no shopping malls. People lived with low expectations. Many could not travel — doctors, officers, engineers and many other professionals, people with no degrees or poor people, were blocked from travelling, except for merchants. People who had to travel needed to pay $400 for each trip outside Iraq, but only after a long procedure waiting for approval to exit the country. Most people could not save that amount. An Iraqi passport is considered to this day as one of the three worst in the world. If one needs a visa to travel to most countries of the world, it's difficult to acquire.

The people who worked in the private sector were getting paid better than those in the public sector, but were still poor, their salaries averaging between $60 and $120 a month.

Even those people considered "middle class" in Iraq, those who owned small businesses or retail shops, continued to operate in old-school ways. There was no chance for an employee to be rich in Iraq. There was no banking system; no credit cards and no loans were available to be leveraged to start a business. If you wanted a loan, maybe only family or friends could help you.

I am fortunate to come from a middle-class family. My parents were both architects, although my father never practiced his profession after his graduation. My mother was employed in her profession and within the last 20 years has designed some of her own projects. Recently she opened her consultancy office and her excellent designs and involvement in designing large projects have helped her become a famous architect in Iraq.

After my father's graduation, for about four years he served his obligatory military service, then started his small stationery business. To this day, he has the same business, still engaged in his one-man-show approach. From the mid-1980s to the early 2000s, we lived primarily on earnings from the stationery business, under a standard considered very good compared with most people in Iraq.

While my father was not a big believer in my skills and never really gave me a proper chance to get involved in his business, in 2008 he asked me for some help to develop his business for him and then in 2009 assigned me to be the general manager of the company after seeing some of my successes as a professional employee in the sales and management field and as a young entrepreneur in various small ventures.

After the 2003 invasion of Iraq, business began to boom. In late 2003, I was at my father's shop. There were a couple of Iraqi traders who owned a retail shop at the airport and were visiting our stationery shop to buy some stationery for their shop. At that time, after the invasion, the airport was one of the largest American bases. The American Army was expressing a high demand for computers and DVDs of movies. Most of the DVDs were pirated, as they still are in Iraq; there is no law providing copyright protection. So those small retail shops did well, asking high prices of the American troops, and getting them.

All my life I'd been passionate about movies and computers, so when I heard those traders mention that they wanted some DVDs for their shop, I jumped in and offered to supply them. Luckily my uncle was a DVD wholesaler so I bought movies from him and supplied them at their office, which is in Baghdad. They then shifted these movies to the airport retail shop. I was making on average $1 profit per movie and selling from 500 to 1,000 movies a day. The shop was making about five to ten times my profit in its pricing to the troops.

Over time they trusted me and liked my style of work with them. One day I saw some computer stuff in their shop ready to be shipped to their airport shop and I asked them if they wanted me to supply them with computer hardware, printers, and other computer devices with better prices. They said yes. I was in touch with the computer market and able to also supply the shop with computer hardware and accessories. I worked with the shop for about five months, after which the owners knew where to locate the main sources for purchasing these items, and developed their own purchasing team.

In less than five months of work as freelance supplier to this retail company, I earned between $40,000 and 50,000 net profit — a very large amount in those days, especially for a 22-year-old guy. At the time, I was still working on my Bachelor's degree at the University of Baghdad, getting my first degree in science, specializing in biology, a subject I never liked and never wanted to understand. It was a mistake choosing this major; I've never found a way to use it or benefit from it.

When my work with the company that was supplying computer accessories and DVDs ended, I was left with about $50,000. I wondered about what to do next. I was passionate about movies, and familiar with the computer market and DVD suppliers, so I decided to open a unique retail shop selling movies and computer software, games and accessories. The shop opened in the first quarter of 2004.

I designed the shop and branded based on my humble experience at the time. It was not perfectly branded, but it was a unique shop with an attractive design and was the first of its kind in Iraq, featuring movies, games and computers. There was no DVD shop in Baghdad holding the same number of movies titles that I had, displayed in the same professional way, by movie categories.

I managed the retail shop and handled all its operations based on the one-man-show concept — handling purchasing, sales and other operations. I had three or four on staff working as salesmen.

The retail shop started succeeding, our sales went up, our product range grew wider, our customer base grew larger, and I started to import computer hardware and accessories items from Dubai and sell wholesale quantities to the wholesale computer market in Baghdad. It was a shift of improvement from retail to wholesale. I briefly changed paths and went to China and developed a speaker product that was branded with the name of my retail shop, and it sold very well in Iraq.

I was always eager to achieve more and always imagined leaving Iraq and moving to another environment that would help me learn, achieve more and thrive. After my first visit to Dubai for one month in July 2005, I fell in love with the city and decided to move there. In November 2005, I made the move. For the next couple of years, I travelled back and forth to Baghdad, exporting items from Dubai to Baghdad, trying to make the system work wirelessly.

By 2007, security in Iraq started to go bad. There were many bombing attacks and kidnapping incidents. Business was getting worse every day, not only because of that but also because I was not qualified to manage a business wirelessly and set a proper system of tracking numbers and employees, because I had built the business on a one-man-show basis, which benefited from my personal supervision. When I moved to Dubai, my employees took over, I was not in control of what was going on, and the business began to fail. In 2007, I shut down the business.

In mid-2006, since my business in Iraq was heading into trouble because a civil war was going on, and also because I was not in control of the business and not equipped with the right skills to manage it remotely, I decided to start over and become an employee in Dubai — starting at zero again. My salary was very low; it barely covered my expenses. It took about a year to become debt-free by selling some of the items left in the shop after closing it and earning a living as an employee.

In Dubai, I experienced a different perspective about professional employment and the corporate world, a world that was new to me. It felt like the right time to leave the small entrepreneurial life behind. I thought that if a small business in Iraq could make $2,000-$4000 a month, and if employment could earn me $4,000-$6000 a month with no headache, with a proper company, that kind of life would be better than the small entrepreneurial life in Iraq. Of course, at that point I was so impressed by the corporate world since we didn't have it in Iraq. I learned a lot from working as an employee in good companies, but over time I started discovering the disadvantages of the corporate world.

At this point, I had worked for several companies as an employee in a variety of industries — from cladding materials (applying one material over another to provide a layer intended to control the infiltration of weather elements, or for aesthetic purposes), paint items, building materials, computer software and hardware products, logistics services and others.

As an employee, I think I was successful. I always followed the system in which I worked, and continuously innovated to find better ways to improve the system and the performance of the companies I worked for. Most of my experience was in sales and business development, starting at the junior level and eventually moving up to managerial positions.

In every environment in which I worked as an employee, I always felt that there was something wrong. As an employee, you might feel unhappy for various reasons — either the salary is not what you'd like, or the company environment is not productive, or management is not up to the standard you would prefer, or you don't have enough authority or the right tools to do your best work. Perhaps you feel that your manager is unfair, not qualified or not treating you well or motivating you to excel in your job. Or maybe you feel that this position is not for you in terms of flexibility, time and control. Could these feelings possibly comprise an entrepreneurial signal — calling you to take action to change your life?

Discovering My Options

"Some people dream of great accomplishments,
while others stay awake and do them."
— Anonymous

I discovered that being an employee was not my only option in life. Those who think this is the only option have likely been raised to believe this by the environment in which they've grown up. If you look around, you'll see that 90% of the people around you are employees. That effect is huge if you don't have mentors to guide you toward a different route.

Sometimes many of us try to change our mindset, change the way we think, but we cannot because we see that everybody around us is doing the same thing. It's fine to spend years learning certain skills that provide you with more options in your life.

Learning to do one thing well can be rewarding. Employees often say, "That's not my job. That's not written into my job description." However, this way of thinking limits you to a small piece of the pie. As we've already discussed, if you wind up losing your job at age 40 or 50, you find yourself in a crisis. When you're young and at entry level, it's easier to find a position like the one you have. The older you become and the more you move up the employee ladder, the more difficult it becomes to find something that matches what you have:

Your expenses increase, and your chances of finding another job that covers your expenses and new lifestyle decrease, especially if the economy is not good. There's almost always a dip in the economy every five to ten years. Also, the stock, real estate, commodities and business markets go up and down. People tend to forget this.

Employees with technical jobs with limited tasks don't know what to do and how to solve problems when they age. Even scholars with PhDs struggle and die poor when they have never been taught how to deal with money or consistent changes. It's important to get out in the real world and try different things. Remember: In a world of dogmatic specialists, it's the generalist who usually ends up running the show. The younger you are, the easier for you to learn and adapt to new situations by pushing yourself out of your comfort zone. When you're younger, your responsibilities and expenses are fewer, you're more active, and motivated to face new challenges and adapt to new risks.

If you spend your life in a business of your own, you continue to build your empire step by step and continue acquiring new skills and techniques. So even if you fail at age 50 or older, you're still likely to get back on your feet, regardless of any emotional effect, because you've been learning all your life in business to deal with different variables. When you manage a business, you know a little about so many different things, while an employee usually knows many details about one particular thing and is less able to deal with unexpected situations. That's why the diversity of intellectual playgrounds breeds confidence instead of fear of the unknown.

If you're an employee, try to begin your work life in sales or marketing. Even if you're working in a different department in your current company, it's easier to ask for a shift to the sales department, because in sales you're going to deal with the real world — learning how to handle rejection, deal with the company internally and customers externally to develop your communication and negotiations skills as well as your emotional intelligence. These skills will help you in all parts of your life whether you are an employee or entrepreneur.

Alternatives to Employment Life

After years of employment in the corporate world, I started realizing its disadvantages. By the end of 2008 and beginning of 2009, I started searching for alternatives to this world by attending seminars and reading more books on personal finance and entrepreneurial approaches. I quit my last job in Dubai in March 2010.

In 2007, my family began living permanently in Dubai because the situation in Baghdad had been very unstable for the past two years. My father was tracking my progress and achievements in the corporate world at the same time his business in Iraq was struggling. His business was dependent on him or his partner being there, but both were living in the UAE at that time.

They decided to use my help in 2008 to work on certain development projects for their accounting system, operations procedures and other tasks. I was working on these wirelessly from Dubai while working my day job, plus studying for my MBA online with the University of Phoenix that I finished in April 2010, so I was under tremendous pressure.

Thankfully I was able to show some results for my family's stationery business. And in January 2009 my father and his partner (my uncle) assigned me to be the general manager of their stationery business. While they previously had given me no opportunity as a teenager to show what I can do in that business, my achievements were now shining brightly in the corporate world. They saw this, they needed help, and they gave me a new chance.

I started putting my full focus on their stationery business, traveled many times between the UAE and Iraq, and developed the business in many ways. It was not easy since the level of resistance to change from the staff and the owners was huge. I was implementing some unfamiliar procedures and they were continually rejecting my processes with "This will not work" or "That will not work in Iraq." But I managed to implement most of the things I wanted. I developed the business, opened some new branches and channels for sales, and made the business more focused on stationery, its core product, even though the owners were branching out into toys, home supplies and various other products.

My father and uncle had been partners in the business since 1984. With different characters and styles of management and goals, they were constantly in conflict but afraid to end the partnership. I started working with them, because I felt that both would do better separately and that it would be best for both families to live in peace. I managed to complete a deal between them on a certain split for the partnership in January 2011 and worked on helping both of them for several months so they could continue working individually. I was more focused on my father but realized that I couldn't properly add more value to the business because he accepted my vision only to a certain extent, likely due to our age gap and his inability to grasp new concepts. Since I felt that I couldn't add more value to him or the business, I decided to resign at the beginning of 2012.

The All in Entrepreneurial Journey

In mid-2011, I started building my first restaurant in Erbil, the capital of Kurdistan, in northern Iraq. The location was in a new mall that was under construction.

We opened in September 2011, the best restaurant in the mall. We did well in the beginning, but the mall was managed badly by inexperienced people; for example, they opened the mall without air conditioning. They made a promise, before the opening, that more than 150 international brands would be represented. After the opening, we discovered this was not true, and all tenants began to struggle.

I started losing money. I had raised some money for this project, but my mother raised a larger amount. Those days were pressure-filled as my family began blaming me for losing money and accusing me of mismanagement of the project. In their opinion, I needed to stay on the premises 12 hours a day. My perspective was to have a franchise business that could run by itself, on autopilot. To this day, my mom doesn't understand the meaning of losing money in an investment that she made because of believing in me, but that's the disadvantage of working with family, because emotions, as discussed, will always affect family relationships.

The failure of this branch was mainly related to the mall traffic, so I started looking for a new location. I found one in the best mall in the city and opened a new branch in March 2012. I raised some of the capital for the new branch from a friend. After being completely broke and psychologically destroyed, thankfully the new branch was extremely successful.

In July 2012, I opened the first branch of my gaming business, Games Corner, which I'm currently expanding as a franchise model. At the time of this writing, I now have thirteen branches. While I hadn't been as inspired by gaming as I had been about the restaurant business, so I did focus more on the restaurant business at the beginning specially after the success of the second branch.

In October 2013, I opened a new branch of the restaurant at Al Ain, the second largest city in the Emirate of Abu Dhabi. Its opening was delayed for more than a year due to a variety of challenges with the contractors, municipality and other parties. First, the contractor was a crook. Legal action was required because we had to bring in another contractor before the mall took the outlet away. This delayed us about four months. While the mall representatives were threatening us with penalties, we were already under pressure from the investor because of the delay. The cost of investment went up because of this delay and because we were paying rent on a space we hadn't yet moved into.

We also had to pay penalties. All of this happened because we'd been penetrating a new market and didn't know any contractor that we'd tested. We had evaluated some contractors, but the ones who were well known were asking more than double the price of those we didn't know. So, we went for a lower price, which was a bad choice.

Sometimes one mistake can lead to many more. We were dealing with a restaurant, which can sometimes face food control issues. The food control and municipality authorities had procedures that weren't clear. Plus, the mall was not familiar with them. We worked based on the mall's knowledge of food control, which, as it turned out, was minimal. When food inspectors arrived, they discovered some areas that did not meet their standards, which delayed our opening another five months.

I talked in more detail about these challenges in my speech about failure at FailCon, which you can watch at beefficient.tv. In essence, the investor/franchisee ran out of money before the opening, and I decided to step in financially to support him. I spent about $150,000 until the end of 2014, when I decided to shut down the project because I couldn't tolerate more losses. Plus, the investor stopped answering my phone calls in June 2014, while at the same time buying time with my financial support. Then, he disappeared. Some court cases are still pending.

The failure of this project was related to the lack of funding from the investor. The location was not properly selected and that was my mistake. There were problems with contractors and many other issues, but, once again, I learned a lot. Problems happen, but you must go on — you have to be patient and strong. You cannot blame anything or anyone, and you need to know, regardless of everything that happens, you can come back and succeed. Some people never try again and, therefore, never succeed.

While I was in the process of ending the nightmare chapter of the UAE restaurant in 2014, ISIS entered Iraq causing huge problems and instability in the north region, resulting in the shutdown of the main road between the middle and northern parts of the country. This caused termination of all business and tourism trips to Erbil, which had depended mainly on Arab tourists coming from the middle and the south parts of Iraq. There was great chaos in Erbil, which devastated our once-profitable restaurant. I tolerated the losses for about a year, and then decided to shut down the branch in May 2015. Hit after hit, lesson after lesson, I kept moving on.

From 2012 to 2015 I have been building a movie ratings app, have participated in some online ventures, opened a couple of gaming branches, plus a branch for a playground for kids. I have also enjoyed some speaking engagements and done some consulting for companies and individuals backed by my blog and web TV show. The rest is history.

Now I'm more focused on expanding my video gaming, kids' amusement and consulting businesses, and taking time to write and add value to other people's lives.

The entrepreneurial journey isn't easy, but it can teach you valuable lessons if you take inspired actions that lead to the priceless rewards of freedom and fulfillment.

CHAPTER 3

WILL YOU BE THE NEXT SUCCESSFUL ENTREPRENEUR?

"What the mind of man can conceive and believe, it can achieve."
— Napoleon Hill

Some people ask me the following question in an attempt to challenge my thoughts, or resist the transition from employee to efficientpreneur. Asking questions is always good. All the steps you want to take in your future begin with challenging questions for yourself and/or others.

The Question I Am Asked Most

The question I am most often asked is: "Should I be a successful employee or an unsuccessful entrepreneur?"

Nobody wants to be unsuccessful, especially in the long run. Our goal is to head toward success. It might be fruitful to be unsuccessful for a while, to learn from the pain – but hopefully only for a short period of time. It's better to experience failure for a brief time than for the rest of your life. Pain and failure are unforgettable teachers. We tend to underestimate them when we are going through them, but later we almost always realize how beneficial they were in helping us turn the corner toward our successful recovery.

Being a successful employee is better than being an unsuccessful entrepreneur but, as we've discussed, there's no guarantee that you're going to always be a successful employee. You may stay limited forever, not necessarily in terms of money but many successful employees quit their high-paying jobs at multinational companies and move to lower-paying situations to enjoy more fulfillment or freedom in their lives.

You need to figure out the challenges and risks of your situation and choose wisely what fits you best. Sometimes circumstances determine what path we take. You don't want to quit your job or stop being a successful employee if you're happy with it.

The world economy is based on a balance of employees and business owners. Entrepreneurs are the ones who create jobs for employees. So the world continually requires more entrepreneurs to solve the unemployment problem, in order to enhance the economy.

According to author and professional speaker Brian Tracy (www.briantracy.com) statistically, in America, more than 74% of wealthy people have made it through self-owned businesses, while only 10% or less of the wealthy have made it as employees, more specifically, as senior executives for big corporations for which they started to work early on, took some stocks options in these companies, and continued climbing their career ladder. Successful self-employed professionals such as doctors or engineers represent less than 10% of the total wealthy people; sales people and sales consultants represent 5%; and the remaining 1% includes inventors, famous authors, singers and successful athletes. According to these statistics, entrepreneurs represent the majority of people who have succeeded in creating wealth. Therefore, you have a greater chance of accumulating wealth as an entrepreneur. That doesn't mean that you can't be wealthy taking the employment path, but being an entrepreneur clearly shows more chance for freedom and wealth.

Creating more alternatives in life gives you peace of mind, so even if you fail in your business, you can figure out another way to go if you know how to plan, sell and raise capital.

If you are a successful employee, you still can learn the skills of being an entrepreneur and make the shift slowly.

Take your time, start small but think big. Making the shift depends on how eager, focused and persistent you are.

What are your visions for your future, and how do you want to spend your life?

Were Some of Us Born Employees?

"You are never too old to set another goal or to dream a new dream."
— C. S. Lewis

Our environment is one of the greatest influences that affect the way we think and make decisions in our careers and in our lives.

When we meet people, sometimes we develop a certain feeling that they've been born to be employees. This idea is based on the moment you see these people and come in contact with their body language, vocabulary and actions. All of these factors are based on how they grew up, the work and home environment in which they lived, and the path they've taken.

When I communicate with new employees who join my businesses, I try to help them adapt entrepreneurial ways of thinking and act as leaders rather than employees to learn how to self-motivate and lead themselves, then lead others. I don't micro-manage them; instead I give them the opportunity to lead and track their performance through numbers and results.

Many of them have come from other company environments and have spent all their lives thinking like employees. I start to teach them step-by-step processes, and give them information they can slowly digest, giving them time to absorb and hopefully adopt new ways of thinking and to act like leaders. I'm so happy to find people smarter than I am in any area of work in my companies, so they can save me time and manage things better than I can.

Many people believe that they've been born to be employees and becoming an entrepreneur is not a choice they can make. The pressure of the crowd and their environment is greater than their will to change and make the transition. One of the most efficient ways to evaluate a person is to dig deeply into his or her family history and business life to develop a much clearer picture of how that person thinks.

The Real Definition of Retirement

If you want to retire at a certain point in your life, now is the right time to aim for it, or certainly within the next 5 to 15 years. When you succeed in implementing your efficient business, you will become financially free, which will allow you to work when you want to work, not because you have to work. Retirement is not meant to be implemented when you're 60 or 70 years old, which is most of the world's perception for retirement. The time to start planning is now.

I don't understand why people would delay their enjoyment of retirement until the end of their lives when they may be barely able to walk. Why don't they retire when they're in their 20s, 30s or 40s? Most people in the world today define retirement as never touching work.

I believe the right definition for retirement is to continue working but work when you want to work, not because you must work.

The current educational or corporate system we see around us does not encourage this definition. The school system is a circle of employees enhanced by our parents and by an environment that continues to feed the same system — around and around it goes. This is why it's often tough for people to break through to the entrepreneurial life.

There is a movement brewing that's focused on creating a new educational system that focuses on entrepreneurial thinking, but it needs work to coincide with what's going on in the real world. Still, it's a step in the right direction. This new movement is still weak, because it's managed by individuals together with small organizations; however, small is the new big with the power of technology and the Internet. Entrepreneurial thinking is growing as more people adopt this process and change the way people think. Much of this is being done via seminars, as well as offline and online courses.

I personally run a similar course by advising individuals to be more efficient in growing their lifestyle businesses and acquire the level of freedom that they have been dreaming about. I'm also working with startups as well as longtime companies to make them work and grow more efficiently. You can visit my website at: www.ahmedalkiremli.com

It's easy to understand why employees often struggle to make the transition from employee to entrepreneur. After 20 or 30 years of being an employee, a person perceives this kind of change as a quantum leap. Other factors include parents, spending 12 years in school, three to six years in a university and then employment for 10 to 20 years. After 30 to 40 years of living in an employee-based world, it's difficult to make the transition if you don't have the right mentors, mindset and tools and aren't persistent enough to make the transition in thoughts and actions. Some master the entrepreneurial life in a few years, but many don't and simply quit. Nobody is born an employee or entrepreneur. Will, actions and environment shape people into who they become.

Does a New Job Give You Security or Freedom?

"If you want total security, go to prison. There you're fed, clothed, given medical care and so on. The only thing lacking...is freedom."
— Dwight D. Eisenhower

Most employees think a new job will give them more security or freedom. The reality is that what they're looking for, and will find, is maybe more security in terms of salary or perhaps a more secure job in the new company with more chance for growth, or a more professional environment or management team. That kind of security might be available for some, but freedom will never be acquired through a job. Maybe you'll feel freer with the new company or work fewer hours, but in general you'll be ruled by specific policies and will need to operate within a certain timeframe, not to mention the politics battles that exist at any company.

Sometimes we believe that getting a new job with higher pay will make us free and able to earn lots of money. Jumping from job to job will not give you freedom. In most cases this is a myth. Even after I've transitioned to being an entrepreneur, from time to time I have still been haunted by the idea of getting a safe, secure job, but over time this idea is fading.

This is what we learned throughout our lives from the people around us. This is what most parents tell their children: Get good grades and be successful in school, so you can get a high-paying, secure job and build your career. This advice worked in the Industrial Age, but is no longer advisable in the Information Age in which we now live. The rules of the game have changed and we need to adapt to them as soon as possible because the rate of change in the Information Age is faster than ever.

The more you follow the employee path, the more you'll believe in it, and the more it will be difficult for you to believe that there's another path to follow in your life to achieve more freedom and security.

How to Get Started

The way to begin is not to quit your job tomorrow, but instead, start planning your exit from your current employment life even if takes you a year, two years or three, or more. It will never happen if you don't make it happen yourself by taking some action. One small action a day will get you there.

If you want to make it into the entrepreneurial life, listen to people who've made it in before you. Those people can mentor you into the proper transition. Get inspired by successful entrepreneurs; read and learn from their biographies, life experiences and mindset. Their journeys will not necessarily be like yours but you can learn from their adventures how to shape yours.

This is the beauty of life, being able to discover new experiences and learn from them. Learn from the people who have been successful at what you are trying to do now. These people are called mentors; they will more efficiently help you implement shortcuts to go from where you are now to where you want to be.

It's fun to learn from a school professor about business but if he or she has never run a business and is still an employee, this is not the right mentor for you. A mentor is someone who has done what you want to do, has gone through actions and challenges, successes and failures that can help you learn.

Freedom is the key to security. When you are free, you have time to think about more productive enterprises, more investment opportunities and time to acquire more knowledge. If all you do is keep looking in the newspaper or online for a job, and jump from one job to another, you'll never be free.

Learn to Read the Numbers

"I've always worked very, very hard, and the harder I worked, the luckier I got."
— Alan Bond

Business people get into trouble when they don't know how to read and interpret the financial aspects of their business, so they don't know what they're getting into and where they're heading. The numbers can cause you sleepless nights, especially if they aren't good. In the short term, it might be a bad thing to know what the numbers are telling you, but it's always good in the long run because you will learn from the mistakes that are shaping the bad numbers and adjust to make the numbers look better in the future. Thinking in the long run is what's going to help you succeed by making the numbers your major guideline for the value of your business. The more value you add, the greater the numbers will follow.

Whether people are employees or entrepreneurs, all too many think that, if they buy a new car, start a new job or new business, everything will be fine, even if they don't know their financials. It is a myth — that everything will go well by itself.

Whether you're managing a business, a family or yourself, understanding and managing your expenses is essential.

Comprehending numbers is the most powerful skill you'll need to master.

The Three Major Financial Records

The income statement, balance sheet and cash flow statement are the three major financial records you need to read and understand to manage your company financials and be able to make better decisions after analyzing the numbers from these three financial reports. These reports will help raise capital from investors and get loans from the bank.

If you understand the concept of these three sheets, you can apply them using an Excel sheet or a more sophisticated accounting program such as Oracle, Quickbooks, Peachtree, Tally or Focus. I personally use simpler statements for my financials generated by Excel, and then my accountants plug in numbers from these statements into the major three. Recently my companies started using Quickbooks online accounting software, which is very good for startups or small to medium size companies. It's easy to generate reports and less complex than Tally or other accounting software.

> **Smart Tip-** I designed an excel spreadsheet to help make your accounting easier. It will help you simplify the details of your expenses, profits, and cash flow. Download your free copy at ahmedalkiremli.com/excel

The balance sheet tells you how much your business is worth. The income statement reflects sales, expenses and profit of your business. The cash flow statement shows you the cash flow situation and the future receivables or payments to or from other parties so you can plan your purchases or investment decisions. Many businesses get stuck because they don't know how to differentiate between the power of income and cash flow. They have so much debt, and don't see that their debt is eating their business alive. More about these later.

Many people make a lot of money from their business or jobs but don't know how to keep it; they don't know where the money is going. They don't have an accountant and don't know how to maintain a budget or forecast their spending. Keeping money is more difficult than making it.

Microsoft Excel

Learn how to use Microsoft Excel. You can't calculate your numbers quickly without putting them into a simple formula that will lead you into more complex formulas that will help you analyze your figures. You can't have a vision for your business without analyzing and understanding those numbers. Learning Excel has changed my life. I've discovered that, as a result, it's easy for me to input my financial numbers, plan a business from zero, and shape my plan and vision based on these numbers.

For my personal financials, to manage daily expenses or the movement of cash between my personal and company accounts, I use a simple app called Home Budget on my iPhone, which I highly recommend. It's critical to know how much you're spending every month. Where is your money going? From which account are you spending? How much do you have on each credit card and in each account? Without numbers, you are blind and it will be impossible to make proper financial decisions.

When people ask me to help them improve the situation of their business in terms of numbers and processes, the first thing I ask for, before touching anything in the business, are the financials. I'll read over the numbers of the last year or two, and those numbers will tell me what's going on and, therefore, how to plan the next steps.

Learning how to read and understand financial information is not rocket science. You can learn it from books or many online or offline courses. Perhaps you know an accountant whom you can invite to lunch and ask about your accounting challenges. Through Upwork.com (formerly Elance), you can hire an accountant online who'll take care of your business, but you need to learn how to read the numbers yourself, to protect yourself and know how to manage your accountants. It's a major requirement for success in your business as well as in your life.

Expenses, Debt and Tax Traps

Most employees, and even some entrepreneurs, struggle with expenses, debt, and tax traps. They stay stuck their entire lives because of these things. Knowing how to manage cash flow and the way you balance your income and expenses is essential in getting out of these traps.

**Knowing how to make money is one thing; knowing
how to manage money, keep your earned money,
and make more of it, is another.**

It's not uncommon to spend all we earn on expenses and/or on debt for mismanagement of loans and mortgages; plus paying taxes — all of which is true even for high-income people. So when we lose a job or stop working for any reason life becomes a disaster because the money flow stops.

Mastering cash flow, knowing how to manage your money and read financial statements is critical for success. The more you get familiar with this, the better off you'll be.

New entrepreneurs often struggle because they know how to use the money they have, but don't always know how to attract and use other people's money (OPM) — from banks, family and friends, angel investors, venture capital, private equity companies and other sources of finance that come under the same umbrella. Raising capital is a major skill to acquire on your entrepreneurial journey.

Employees usually pay more taxes than entrepreneurs; the more they earn, the more taxes they pay. Not all entrepreneurs know how to make tax-free money because they don't hire the right tax experts or lawyers to help them. While that sounds expensive, in reality they end up paying more in taxes than what they pay those experts. Nowadays, you can use the power of outsourcing online to consult experts for a reasonable hourly rate.

The Rat Race

The rat race is an endless, pointless, self-defeating process of repeating certain actions, much like the life of some employees.

Most often, employees wake up in the morning, have a quick breakfast, rush-feed the kids if they have any, drop them off at school quickly, then dash quickly to work to arrive at 9 a.m., grabbing their morning coffee. Then they work two to three hours, keep looking at their watches to count the minutes until lunch time, sometimes stretching their hour lunch to 90 or 120 minutes. They return to work for a couple of hours, chat with colleagues, work a bit more, then spend the rest of the time planning when to leave work.

Other employees kill themselves working an extra two to three hours because they are workaholics or hope to achieve a promotion. After they leave work they are stuck in traffic because of rush hour, then reach home in one to three hours, based on traffic and distance. During weekdays, they often don't have time for family, sports or entertainment because they're exhausted from their work routine and always under stress to keep their job by strictly following the policies and politics of the company and doing their best to be nice to people they'd rather not be nice to.

They have a quick dinner with the family; sometimes the kids are asleep by that time, so they chat or argue with their spouse. Then they go to sleep, and the next day they get up and do it all again. At the end of the week, they start counting the hours to reach the weekend.

"The trouble with being in the rat race is that even if you win, you're still a rat."
— *Lily Tomlin*

The weekend arrives, they do some shopping, then hang out with the family, entertain the kids, and many of them get drunk to forget the tiring week that they've gone through. This same process is repeated their entire life as they hope life will change by itself, but it doesn't. It doesn't until they get a wakeup call due to a disaster or from a revolution that comes from within them. The fact is, you don't have to wait for a disaster. It's never too late to start over again.

This is the rat race of far too many employees. It's one of my goals to help more people become aware that they're caught in this routine, as many of them don't discover it until they are much older.

Sometimes when I wake up early, I see the rat race in the morning at 8 o'clock as all cars are going to work at the same time, the traffic is horrible, and my brain draws a picture of too many rats leaving their homes and running in the direction of their cheese. This image repeats between 5 p.m. and 7 p.m. when employees are traveling home from work.

I often go to malls to eat, work, interview somebody, go to the bank, watch a movie or shop, but I try my best to avoid weekends in the malls because the heavy traffic brings the same rats there, when you must struggle to park or simply enjoy your shopping experience. I try to plan my visits to the malls on weekdays when most employees are still at work.

It's important to diagnose the rat race that you're in, and then act to escape it.

Employee Excuses for Not Going Entrepreneurial

"Don't say you don't have enough time. You have exactly the same number of hours per day that were given to Helen Keller, Pasteur, Michelangelo, Mother Teresa, Leonardo da Vinci, Thomas Jefferson, and Albert Einstein."
— H. Jackson Brown

Lack of Time

Usually lack of time is one of the major excuses people express for not going entrepreneurial. Most people complain about not having enough time because they don't know how to manage their time, how to plan and prioritize to get more things done to achieve their dreams and relax later on. They prefer to stay in the rat race forever instead of sacrificing a couple of hours a day for a certain period of time.

Everybody is busy nowadays with what I consider noise — Facebook, television, and other mainstream media channels that drain your brain and reduce your productivity. You'll have enough time if you know how to plan and create that time, how to set goals and focus on executing important things rather than draining your time because of the noise around you.

Since the year 2010 I decided to stop watching TV because it's one of the greatest sources of noise and wastes of my time. If there's something I'd like to watch, I'd rather use my computer, go onto the Internet, and watch whatever I want to watch at any time instead of waiting for my favorite show, which half the time is spent on ads. Just about anything is available via such services as YouTube, Vimeo, Netflix, iTunes, Apple TV and others. Spend less time, and less money.

I do have a large TV at home that I use to connect with my computer screen when I want to watch a specific movie or show, or study a certain presentation. I'm not suggesting that you eliminate entertainment time from your life; sometimes we need a couple of hours a day to relax and watch something to get more relaxed and help us be more productive later. If you watch TV, just become more aware of your viewing habits.

Time is one of the most precious things in this life, so use it wisely. It's the only currency that's irreversible.

One of the greatest struggles for most people is using time efficiently. There is nothing worse than wasting time on the wrong project. Go to www.ahmedalkiremli.com/tools to get my secret weapon for efficiency in life and business.

I Am Busy

The point of being busy is that your brain is focused on one thing and usually that thing will remedy a short-term pain or solve a problem. It's fine to focus on one thing for a long-term, fruitful outcome such as being financially free within five years, but not a short-term one to cure your pain temporarily while the big-picture problem exists forever, although this is how most employees are taught.

Everybody is busy nowadays but it's best to keep yourself busy with important things rather than urgent things, or at least create a logical balance between the important and urgent that will lead you to the outcome you want, where you can add the most value and get the most level of fulfillment.

I Want It to Be Perfect

While thinking of many of the products, brands or services I wanted to launch, I remember that I always wanted to be perfect and ended up spending months, and then later quitting the project. As a result, I learned how to create a process of steps, how to then test each step, go to the next step and look for excellence rather than perfection.

I wanted to create a movie ratings app, which I did and which you can find at www.BestMovieRatings.com, or download it from the app store by searching Best Movie Ratings. I hired a developer and gave him the idea to execute. After more than two months of back-and-forth discussions, he failed to deliver what I wanted and quit. One of the reasons was that my idea was difficult for any developer to digest. So, I decided to simplify it by giving the developer a small feature to execute first. After he succeeded, I then asked him to implement a more complex feature – how to build a complex formula on an Excel sheet. This process has to start simply then get more complex after each step because each step builds on the previous implemented step. This is the same with developing any new technology; it must go through stages of development.

When I communicated with the second developer I didn't overwhelm him with the entire process. We developed it step by step and it worked. Unfortunately, after he reached a certain stage, the source code was stolen. Once again, I was back at zero, but at least I had gained some knowledge on how to simplify the app and how to create an agreement with a third developer.

In order not to face a similar issue with the source code, I hired the third developer using the knowledge that I had acquired from the previous two experiences and provided a more secure agreement. Now things have worked and the app has been developed in a way that has exceeded my expectations. With each new version, we're improving the app and adding more features that had never been planned before. At the date of this writing, we continue to develop it.

It's always advisable to build any project based on what I call the Excel formula, one step at a time. Then, once it's set, it will lead you to another more complicated and sophisticated version.

Employees often fail to create something outside their job because they think that they need to perfect it. The best approach is to simplify the idea, take it step by step, and launch it on a small scale. Once that's achieved, then it's time to improve it and scale it. Start small and think big.

Steve Jobs said, "Real artists ship." What he meant is that everyone has ideas, but "real" artists deliver on them before they are perfectly ready because there's no such thing as perfect. Apple would "ship" its new product in a simple format, await feedback, then keep improving it. Many large companies today continue to keep improving "bugs" in their new products. Now it's common practice, especially in the technology sector, because this sector moves so fast. You need to ship fast and improve fast because there's no time to perfect things. When you ship, you'll quickly learn what your clients want. Then you give it to them in the next version. This process made customer response an essential part of Jobs' process.

I Have a Family

You have a family, you have children, and you have a lot of expenses. You can't quit your job and risk losing pay. The fact is you can become an entrepreneur without quitting your job by having a part-time situation, building your online or offline business after work, or sharing a partnership with someone or working on a side project that can be your full-time project one day. All you need to do is start allocating one to two hours a day or one to two days a week to your dream idea or side project. Use that time to take small actions. You will realize that the accumulation of those small actions become something impressive. Having a family will not block you from managing your time more efficiently and realizing your dreams.

You may need to struggle at the beginning, working longer hours, but keep in mind that you'll have time to enjoy later. Otherwise, you'll spend your life fearing losing your job. You risk more by living endlessly in that state of mind.

I Don't Have the Skills

Are you an employee who believes that you don't have enough skills to take on a project or venture, or don't have enough skills to change your life? Skills can be learned with time, proper planning, appropriate mentors, a positive mindset, and by taking action. We live in the Information Age. Any information you desire is there for anything you want to learn. Thanks to the Internet, it is easier to find the right books and best mentors — and to study any project or idea from a variety of perspectives, which was impossible before the Internet arrived. Leverage the power of the Internet! Develop skills to deliver your project.

These days the Internet can even help you outsource a team to deliver your project, on your behalf, faster and at a lower cost. I have used Elance to outsource most of my online teams, but there are many other services out there, such as www.Odesk.com. Now Elance and Odesk have merged into one service called www.Upwork.com. Also: www.Guru.com, or 99design.com. You don't need to have all the skills necessary for delivering your project — you just need to learn how to lead your team to execute the project on your behalf. You can use the Internet as your dashboard or operations room. Start small, think big, and work on simple ideas that require a small team and low budget. For example, you might develop a website or app online, or a kiosk project offline to add value to a certain number of customers. Think value, and the money will follow.

I Am Not Smart Enough

What does it mean to be smart? Look at the most successful entrepreneurs. Are they smart? They are focused on what they do best and are persistent in executing their ideas and projects, even if they fail.

I had always thought that failure is a bad thing, because that's what the school system and environment in which I lived taught us. Later I learned that failure is one of the most important factors in the formula of success, so now I approach failure as an opportunity to learn more. I mention this many times, because it's important for you to believe it. It's painful at the time the failure is happening, but later, when you look back, you notice that the experience you gained was priceless. With time, you learn that if you can face a new failure, you know that you'll survive it, and learn from it. With more time and more failures, you'll get stronger and more experienced, so that you'll be able to go through painful experiences more successfully.

You don't need to be a genius to be a successful entrepreneur; you just need to create a successful formula and keep repeating it.

I Am Too Old

Kentucky Fried Chicken founder Colonel Harland Sanders (1890-1980) started KFC when he was 66 years old. In the early days of his life, he worked at many different low-paying jobs. He was a blacksmith's helper, cleaning out ash pans of trains, a fireman, and insurance salesman. He started selling fried chicken from his roadside restaurant in Corbin, Kentucky, during the difficult days of the Great Depression. Later he identified the potential of franchising his restaurant and opened the first KFC franchise in Utah in 1952. In that year Colonel Sanders was 62 years old. In 1955, when he was 65 years old, he started travelling the United States to franchise his own secret chicken recipe to independent restaurant owners. They would pay four to five cents on each chicken as a franchise fee, in exchange for his secret blend of herbs and spices and the right to feature his recipe on their menus.

In 1959, when he was 69 years old, he opened the company headquarters in Shelbyville; and in 1964 when he was 74 years old, he sold part of the franchise company to a group of investors for $2 million. The company then sold multiple times to different investors and companies, and the last company to acquire KFC was PepsiCo in 1986 for $850 million (equivalent to around 1.8 billion in 2013). The point is to never give up, and that you're never too old to become an entrepreneur.

I Don't Have Enough Money

Money and investment are big issues employees face when they want to pursue their entrepreneurial dream. Today, there are many ways to solve this problem. Many startups raise millions of dollars when the founder or cofounders master the process of pitching their idea to angel investors or venture capitalists. I suggest that you start with a small project that doesn't require a lot of money, such as an Internet business, an app or a small offline kiosk. Remember, if you can't convince your family or close friends to invest in your idea, it will be difficult to pitch it to other investors. Pitch your idea to the right investors or use banks to fund your idea. Many times I used my credit card to fund some of my small projects — such as www.gamescorner.com, which I'm currently expanding.

So, in summary, start somewhere, launch your product or idea, keep improving and adjusting it — learn from your mistakes to create the best product or service possible. Finally, fail fast when you feel things are not working the way you want, so you can start over with something else without wasting time on something that does not work. Your success begins when you start admitting and learning from your mistakes.

"Studies show that people are terrible at estimating their abilities. Recently, we set out to see who is most likely to do this. Sure, we found that people greatly misestimated their performance and their ability.

But it was those with the fixed mindset who accounted for almost all the inaccuracy.

The people with the growth mindset were amazingly accurate. When you think about it, this makes sense. If, like those with the growth mindset, you believe you can develop yourself, then you're open to accurate information about your current abilities, even if it's unflattering."

— Carol S. Dweck

Can You Be the Next Successful Entrepreneur?

Can everyone be an entrepreneur? Many people ask this question and the answer is: yes…and no. The answer is yes, if you:

- Have the right mindset.
- Have the ability to create a vision for the business.
- Are persistent and keep fighting to achieve your goals.
- Are strong enough to not quit your dream.
- Have a presentable and credible character.
- Are not influenced by ongoing negative feedback from your family and friends.
- Are determined to develop your self, business and life.
- Have the ability to manage your emotions.
- Can make the right decisions at the right time.
- Are a positive, optimistic person.
- Have good communication and negotiating skills.
- Know how to sell and market.
- Analyze the numbers, hire the right people, provide the best customer service, conduct the right market research, know how to raise capital and pitch the right source of capital.
- Understand the legal regulations that surround your business.
- Have Internet marketing experience, social media knowledge, and know how to stay ahead of the competition and improve your business market share.
- Can manage cash flow.

- Know what to do during disasters, and cope with stress that comes from challenges you are going to continuously face as a business owner, or investor — and overcome.

You are overwhelmed now, right?

The reality is that you need the above-mentioned skills to become a successful entrepreneur, but not necessarily all of them. You can learn most of them with time and experience, but you need to be persistent enough to do so.

To start you need two primary elements — a goal and the persistence to achieve that goal.

Anything in between is achievable, because you're motivated to accomplish the needed skills to achieve your goal.

The answer is no, if you:

- Don't have the right mindset.
- Consciously make excuses.
- Are negative about everything around you.
- Don't want to take any risk so you end up with bigger risks because you don't know how to manage the risk.
- Follow the advice of friends or family when they give you advice you don't want or need.
- Believe people who think you are a loser.
- Can't handle stress.
- Are too lazy to explore what's outside your comfort zone.
- Don't believe in yourself.

Are you resistant enough, or do you want to go for the easy solution of having a job, which is short-term pain relief for your fears and problems? Could it be, that in the long term, that job could be the greatest risk snowball you've built over many years — one that, someday, will destroy your life with no ultimatum?

Are Entrepreneurs Born or Are They Made?

One of my favorite inspirations about luck is the story of Soichiro Honda (1906-1991). He was born in a small village and spent his early years helping his father with his bicycle repair business. Soichiro was not a fan of traditional education. His school was always asking him to stamp his grade reports from his family with the family seal to make sure that his family was aware of how low his grades were. He solved this problem by making his own seal from a used rubber bicycle pedal. His seal was discovered by school management when he started to make forged stamps for other students.

When he was 15, he went to Tokyo and secured an apprenticeship at a garage in 1922 where he worked for six years. He didn't much like the idea of being employed, and headed back to his hometown to start his own auto repair business in 1928. Like many other countries, Japan was hit badly by the Great Depression of the 1930s. Honda started a little workshop, developing the concept of the piston ring. His plan was to sell the idea to Toyota. He labored night and day, even slept in the workshop, always believing he could perfect his design and produce a worthy product. He was married by now, and pawned his wife's jewelry for working capital.

Finally, he completed his piston ring and was able to take a working sample to Toyota, only to be told that the rings did not meet their standards. Soichiro went back to school and suffered ridicule when the engineers laughed at his design. He refused to give up. Rather than focus on his failure, he continued working toward his goal. After two more years of struggle and redesign, he won a contract with Toyota.

The Japanese government was gearing up for war. With his contract in hand, Soichiro needed to build a factory to supply Toyota, but building materials were in short supply. Still he would not quit. He invented a new concrete-making process that enabled him to build the factory. In 1937 Honda founded Tokai Seiki Heavy Industry, to manufacture piston rings for Toyota.

With the factory now built, he was ready for production. His plant was bombed twice during World War II. A United States B-29 bomber destroyed Tokai Seiki's Yamashita Plant in 1944. Mr. Honda started collecting surplus gasoline cans discarded by U.S. fighters – "gifts from President Truman," he called them, which became new raw materials for his rebuilt manufacturing plant. Finally, an earthquake destroyed the factory and the Itawa plant collapsed in the 1945 Mikawa earthquake.

Was this the end of the road for Honda? Of course not. He sold the salvageable remains of his company to Toyota and founded the Honda Technical Research Institute in 1946. After the war, an extreme gasoline shortage forced people to walk or use bicycles. Honda built a tiny engine and attached it to his bicycle. His neighbors wanted one, and although he tried, materials could not be found, so he was unable to supply the demand. In 1948, he found materials and started producing complete motorized bicycles.

Honda wrote to 18,000 bicycles shop owners and, in an inspiring letter, asked them to help him revitalize Japan. Some 5,000 responded and advanced him what little money they could to build his tiny bicycle engines. Unfortunately, the first models were too bulky to work well, so he continued to develop and adapt, until finally, the small engine "Honda Super Cub" became a reality and was a success. With success in Japan, Honda began exporting his bicycle engines to Europe and America.

In the 1970s there was another gas shortage, this time in America. Automotive fashion turned to small cars. Honda was quick to pick up on the trend. Experts now in small engine design, the company started making tiny cars, smaller than anyone had seen before, and rode another wave of success.

"Tough times never last, but tough people do."
— Dr. Robert H. Schuller

Honda Corporation is now one of the largest automobile companies in the world. Honda succeeded because he was persistent enough to keep trying, regardless of the bad luck and obstacles he had faced during his career, and turned whatever bad luck into a learning experience that transformed into a successful opportunity. He is a great lesson on achieving your dreams.

Luck is often involved in processes, projects or goals that wind up successful but, at the end of the day, it's your dedication, persistence and stubbornness to achieve your goals that feed that luck.

You need to be lucky only one time, at the right time, to be called lucky for the rest of your life.

More than ten years ago, I was a very negative person and always felt I'd been unlucky. My parents were not supporting me, many things were not going the way I wanted, and whatever project or goal I went after, I approached with a negative spirit. I would start a project as a loser before ever starting the journey. Negativity can be a kind of snowball that you need to melt at a certain point in your life.

When I was in first grade, my mother used to give me chocolate, some fruit and a sandwich when I went to school, or some money to buy what I wanted from the school shop. When I did something she considered "naughty" at home, she would stop giving me money for a week or so.

When I came home from school the next day, she saw that I had even more stuff than what she had given me. She used to search my bags when I came home from school. When she saw that I had a lot of stuff, she got worried and asked me, "Where did you get all of these things? Tell me!" I told her, "You know what? I don't need you anymore, and I can take care of myself." She shouted again, "Where did you get this stuff?" So, I told her. My father and uncle used to be partners in their stationery business. They had misprinted stickers and posters that they didn't want. I still remember that some of these posters were printed with cartoon characters, but there were some issues with the printing, so I asked if I could take them. They gave these to me, and I took some of these big posters and stickers and sold them to some kids at the school. As I told my mother, she started smiling. To this day, whenever I have any entrepreneurial success, she tells this story when people ask how I became an entrepreneur.

I believe that I was born an entrepreneur. Still, I learned to become a professional one by practicing, learning, creating, experimenting, testing and correcting. Some people are born with the entrepreneurial character, but it's not enough. You still need to train and practice. Other people are born with nothing and they still can become entrepreneurial with the right amount of practice, experience, mentors and other sources of learning.

"Success is walking from failure to failure with no loss of enthusiasm."
— Winston Churchill

CHAPTER 4

WHAT YOU NEED FOR YOUR ENTREPRENEURIAL JOURNEY

"If you think you are beaten, you are. If you think you dare not, you don't. If you want to win, but think you can't, it's almost a cinch you won't. If you think you'll lose, you're lost; for out in the world, we find success begins with a fellow's will; it's all in the state of the mind. Life's battles don't always go to the stronger and faster man, but sooner or later, the man who wins is the man who thinks he can."
—Walter D. Wintle

Your mindset is a combination of a number of things: your mental attitude, action or reaction to certain situations, problems or outcomes.

Everything starts with your perspective — how you look at things. Developing your mindset is the first step in aiming for success as an entrepreneur. It's the core source of your decision-making process in solving any problem and creating the path for your vision.

Create a Proper Mindset, Then Take Action

The difference between successful people and unsuccessful people consists of only two factors: mindset and actions. Your way of thinking determines how you learn, how you select your investment path, how you look at the world and where you want to be. Succeeding in business is about knowing how you're going to tackle issues you need to face on your way to achieving anything.

Having a positive mindset is a major qualification for your success with anything or anyone. Having a dream that comes from a positive attitude is what helps set your goal and work toward it. All successful entrepreneurs have it.

A decade ago, I was the most negative person on Earth. It was a huge barrier to my success. I thought that any failure I faced was related to my bad luck and always felt I was the targeted person — the marked loser. When you start changing your mindset and hanging out with positive people, your mindset shifts.

The books I've read, mentors I've spent time with, experience I've garnered — they've all taught me how to think positively.

Because you're going to face problems, self-doubt and criticism from others, you need to build yourself a foundation of positive thinking. Failures need to be tackled with a positive attitude.

You *can* practice positive thinking and train your mind to think positively. Listen to your inner voice and believe what it's saying to you. It's essential to believe in yourself and develop the confidence that will help you achieve great things.

Any failure needs to be categorized as an opportunity to learn. You need to trust that, in the face of any failure, you have the power to come back.

Your Most Important Asset

It's common to think that money or other tangible possessions are the most important assets in business. We don't realize that the most essential asset is your brain and the way your mind operates.

Your brain is the source of all your successes, all your failures and whatever decisions you make throughout your life. The information and knowledge that develop in your brain determine what's going to shape your decisions, set the channels toward anything you want to achieve in your life, where you're going to live, the lifestyle you're going to pursue, and the happiness you're going to desire and achieve.

If you lose all your money, you can make it back if you have a brain equipped with the right knowledge. If you infect your brain with negative or wrong information, you're going to suffer all your life. So, you need to be aware of what you choose to put in your brain along with the influences that affect it, such as friends, environment and other sources of knowledge. Keep in mind that not all sources of information are necessarily good or healthy for you or your brain.

Knowledge is something we acquire, not something we're born with. Most successful people we see started from scratch. Personal development is a remarkable path that many people don't discover, but once they do, they rarely stop working on themselves. It's a kind of addiction — a positive one.

I used to make fun of people who liked to read. Since I discovered my path of personal development by reading books, attending seminars, learning from mentors and others, my life changed. Day after day, the more I learn, the more powerful I feel. I've discovered many things about myself as well as the value I can contribute to this world.

When you know where to find the right knowledge and how to use it, you can do anything you want. You can be happy. You can be rich. You can live with more satisfaction. Whatever you want to know about or accomplish is waiting for you to discover. This path is unbelievably simple. Once you take this personal development journey, you'll never stop, you'll always be hungry to learn more, to achieve more goals. You'll find that your goals will shift, as will your desire to affect the lives of people around you.

> **Your main goal is not to achieve many goals, but to feel fulfilled. Fulfillment will lead you to happiness.**

Don't be greedy with your knowledge. Invest in it! It's not that costly compared to many things you spend money on in your life. The cost of a book, audio book or seminar is not as costly as you think, and any one of them might change your life forever.

This is my advice to you, even if you're physically disabled: Use the Internet. Current technology can provide you with the power to be fulfilled, to achieve and to add to the community and society in which you live — more than ever. Even if you can't walk, you can still achieve a great deal.

I began this book by speaking some parts of it because, for me, it's faster. Then, I sent my recording to a transcriber who transcribed the vocal dictation into text. My next step was to review the text, revise anything necessary, and then send to an editor for a final review. You can achieve a lot these days with only your brain, a computer and an Internet connection.

I'm not scared of losing money. Of course, the less the loss, the easier it is to come back. I know now, regardless of the damage, situation or challenge I face, I can always make it back because I feel that I've developed the mindset and knowledge I need to bring me back. I know the paths to take; I have the desire and am persistent enough to come back.

> **This combination — developing knowledge, being persistent, being passionate about your work, and taking action — will bring you back, no matter how much trouble you face or how great the problem.**

Most people are not prepared when opportunity knocks. You need to have a vision, a desire to learn, the desire to equip yourself with the right skills and be ready to take focused, consistent action. Then, when the opportunity comes, you're ready.

Fixed Mindset and Growth Mindset

A fixed mindset is one in which intelligence is static. You avoid the full potential of your mindset by avoiding any new development and sticking with your current status. A growth mindset is one in which you're open to growth and learning to reach for the unlimited power of thought and success. A fixed mindset can become a growth mindset. All it takes is a desire and tendency to learn new things.

Carol Dweck, a Ph.D. professor at Stanford, discusses a comparison between fixed and growth mindsets in her book, *Mindset: The New Psychology of Success*[3] in terms of challenges, effort, criticism and success of others.

People with a fixed mindset, when facing challenges, want to perform well and look smart. Challenges stop them from achieving what they want. The fixed mindset sticks to the status quo, because that's what that mind knows. The desire is to avoid failing and avoid the negative impact that might affect self-image.

People with a growth mindset embrace challenges because they believe they will come out stronger because of the challenge. They persist in the face of setbacks and obstacles, and approach failure as an opportunity to learn new things and adjust to future challenges.

Obstacles Are Challenges

When people with a fixed mindset face obstacles, they usually give up easily because they experience an external force that pushes them out of their comfort zones. They envision any extra effort as fruitless, because after working toward certain goals and having to return to square one, they feel they have achieved nothing.

---

[3] Dweck, Carol. *Mindset: The New Psychology of Success.* NY: Ballatine Books, 2006.

Growth mindset people are persistent when they face obstacles and setbacks. They believe in the potential of their goals so they try harder, do their best and continue to hope for success. Failure never discourages them from trying to achieve their goals or new outcomes.

Those with a fixed mindset think that the smart thing is to dispense with effort because it doesn't help.

The growth mindset sees effort as the path to mastery, one that will lead to future growth. It believes that more work is required to master useful skills that will lead to greater growth and success.

Criticism Can Be Helpful

People with a set mindset tend to ignore negative feedback, even when it's useful. They believe that criticism of their work is a criticism of them. This tends to discourage supportive people from providing any negative feedback. This results in isolating the fixed-mind person from external influences and limiting resources that might be beneficial.

Growth mindset people approach criticism as a way of learning, a way of correcting their path and learning from it. They look at criticism as feedback to improve and thrive. They believe that negative feedback is not a threat to their dream but something that will help them reshape their approach in a better way.

Success of Others

Fixed mindset people see the success of others as a personal threat and try to ignore or devaluate it by arguing that the source of this success is a matter of pure luck. It's difficult for them to achieve what others have achieved, so they sometimes point to negative factors the successful person used to have, to draw a negative picture of the successful person.

Growth mindset people approach success stories of others as an inspiration to their own success.

Any employee who dreams of transitioning to efficient entrepreneur needs to think in the growth mindset way. You can shift your way of thinking by diagnosing and admitting that you have a fixed mindset mentality. That's a necessary first step. Then you can start to listen to your fixed mind, and track it. Become aware of your actions and fears, and come up with alternate paths to change the way you think about your fears. The choice to change is yours. You are not forced to stick with your fixed mindset — you can let it go. The process may take time. The more you take a growth mindset action, the sooner you develop a growth mindset way of thinking.

Open your mind to learn from failures and to approach them as opportunities.

It's common to have negative thoughts because of the challenges and obstacles that surround us from time to time. Every human has ups and downs. Knowing how to use those thoughts to get to positive thoughts is what you want to learn. Any current disaster you're living through is an opportunity to learn how to become smarter and stronger in the future. Succeeding in transforming your negative thoughts into positive ones will have a huge impact on your daily life.

You may not necessarily transform all of your thoughts positively, but in time you will develop the habit and notice that your attitude in general will become more positive. People around you will start telling you that they see a significant change in your character. They may not be able to express what exactly they're seeing, but you will know what it is.

I played for the Iraqi National Squash Team for more than ten years. I was ranked No.1 some of those years. At the day of this writing, I'm still active and play in the Dubai League and other tournaments in the United Arab Emirates and other countries. There are times when I enter the squash court with a negative mindset by filling my brain with excuses or negative thoughts, such as: I am overweight, I am a bit old, I have a problem with my knee, I didn't sleep well yesterday, I ate a lot at lunch that I shouldn't eat when I have a match. With thoughts like these, my brain keeps creating excuses for me to lose, and that's what usually happens; I end up losing the match, sometimes to weaker players.

When I focus on the strengths I have in the game, and enter with a clear mindset, focused on winning and giving the best performance possible by fighting to win each point, the outcome is different. The same applies to life.

Positive people are well liked; they make people around them happy. Nobody likes to be around negative people. Positive people achieve outstanding performances because of their attitude and the energy that explodes from their bodies. We sometimes fall in love with stage performers because of the positive energy they exude, which is a large part of their show. Be like them! Train yourself and your brain to be positive regardless of the situation.

Negative people radiate anger from their bodies. They feel miserable and unlucky most of the time, and believe the world is against them. Most often they are in bad health and exist in high stress situations that they themselves have created. As a result, they represent a liability for society rather than an asset. Pull yourself out of their league.

It appears to be true that what you think is what you get. You must program your brain to erase all the viruses that are infecting your brain with negative thoughts, and transform them into thoughts that reflect your dream, goals and longed-for achievements.

Contemplate Solutions Instead of Fears

In addition to being positive, you need to be realistic with your decisions. Always write down ten solutions for the problem you are facing and act to solve it by doing your best and hoping for the best. Nothing in life is guaranteed. You might die tomorrow but that doesn't mean you shouldn't be optimistic about what's coming next.

Sometimes we isolate ourselves to focus on what we want to achieve. We may experience many lonely moments when we feel we're alone in this world — we feel scared and hopeless. This is a normal feeling. It happens regardless of how successful we are. Many times these thoughts will invade your brain, and when they do, you must focus and release your brain from these thoughts, perhaps by doing something you like — playing sports, getting a massage, jogging and breathing in some good air, or going to the cinema. Seeing a good movie transforms my thoughts and my mood. So does playing squash or hanging out with some friends, or working on a project I'm passionate about.

You can read motivational quotes or books about happiness or transforming bad habits into good ones. If you have diagnosed the problem properly, you can find a solution for it — one you can start tackling.

You need to choose to be happy. If that's not your normal state of mind, it takes time to train your brain. You need to look at the bright side of life and stay optimistic regardless of challenges, and find more reasons to smile as much as you can.

Hang out with happy people; keep them around you. Stop spending time with negative people. Personality is always affected by environment. When people live in countries going through war, their negative environment always makes them feel sad and fearful.

Sometimes we need to change our environment to inspire ourselves to change. Every day, take time to visualize a bright light at the end of the tunnel.

Practice Humility

Ego is a Latin word meaning "I." It is also a Greek word, also meaning "I." Your ego can be your worst enemy, one that's often hidden.

One of the biggest obstacles we find in life is our self. The way we think, sometimes after succeeding in a project or venture, grows into a feeling of superiority. We think that nobody can beat us in anything now and our ego skyrockets. When this happens, our learning stops. We believe that we don't need to learn more and that we've already figured out everything we need to know.

When you get onto the path of learning and personal development, you realize that the more you learn, the humbler you become. We are nothing in this universe without adding value to it, and to add value we need to have knowledge that can come only through learning.

The more you learn, the more helpful you'll be to others because you will continually work toward adding value to people besides yourself. The more value you add to others, the more people will hunger for the value you provide.

Do your best to give as much as you can before you ask for something in return. The best thing is to give without asking for anything in return. This is a great way to claim your authority and drive your image or brand. Many people volunteer for charity work because they know that when they give to this world, the world often rewards them back. Take some time to stop thinking about yourself as the main priority and think about adding value to others. Even when you want to create a new product, the first thing you need to think of, to make your product successful, is how it's going to add value to others, because only by adding value to others will your product be successful.

Ego can lead you into dark areas that you may not discover until years later. It can make you lose many valuable assets —family, friends, and credibility. It can leave you alone with no support from others and create massive failure in areas you never expected.

None of us knows all the answers for everything in this world, so the best advice is to stay humble and keep learning. The more you learn, the more humble and confident you will become.

Handle Tough Times

"It's fine to celebrate success but it is more important to heed the lessons of failure."
— Bill Gates

During your life, you're going to face tough times. As you transition from employee to efficient entrepreneur, you'll face even tougher times, regardless of whether or not you know what you're going to do.

Sometimes we need to risk, just get started, and see how things will go. It's important to learn how to manage your risk, or at least calculate it, to see how much damage you're going to face. You will never calculate the damage perfectly, but the more projects you do, the better you'll become at calculating expectations. If you're new at what you're doing, be sure to consult with people who've done what you are trying to do, before you jump in.

In one of my projects I hired a contractor who didn't start the project work for three-and-a-half months. He requested and got a 25% down payment, but didn't touch the project despite the fact that the agreement clearly stated that he would deliver the project in 45 days. Every day he had a new excuse, such as mall approval, municipality approval, food control approval, struggles with his suppliers. Every delay cost me money, because I had to pay rent to the mall, and salaries to the staff while they were undergoing training. The contractor didn't pay the penalties stated in the contract, so I took legal action.

After three months, I started negotiating with a new contractor to replace the first one. The new contractor took advantage of the process by pricing us higher than the first, because he knew the disaster we had experienced with the first contractor, and knew that time was costing us money. We didn't have time to find better prices, because we were under pressure from the mall to either take the outlet from us, or pay the rent. We had already paid so much that we couldn't afford to back off the project.

Problems happen, and sometimes reach worst-case scenarios you never anticipate. Sometimes when you start a new project and you don't have much credibility, or your brand is still new, you cannot plug contingency plans into your business plan for one to two years, because the investment will be much greater. That will make most of the investors run away. When I start, I record the "cost until we open the project" as the needed capital to open and clearly mention to investors that they will bear losses if a project fails.

New, small investors are easily scared and could leave the project on your shoulders, even if you have a contract with them stating that they're the ones responsible for any losses. If they do depart, your only resort is to take legal action, which will take time and money. So, you start paying losses from your pocket, because offline projects cannot be stopped anytime you wish, and continued after you raise another round of funding, because for offline projects, you're paying for employees, rent and interior and exterior decoration.

When you are starting out and working with friends and/or family as investors, you can't anticipate extra costs on the project. This would scare them and make the process of raising capital for your dream more difficult. But this doesn't mean that you must lie about the costs of the project; you just need to be honest in reporting that the capital you're raising from them will be used only to start the project.

The timing is never right to start something new, so you need to push yourself and just start your project. Personal, life and business problems never end. You'll always be short of money; you'll always have family problems. All you can do is choose the best possible timing.

Plan as much as you can but don't delay since this will delay your learning and your breakthrough. Make the move and get ready to risk. Try as much as you can to minimize the risk. Sometimes the pressure of the process that you are going through is the best teacher. Some of the best moments I enjoy are seeing other people's breakthrough moments.

When you fail, it's the greatest learning experience you'll have. Just know that it's okay to fail — all of us fail at certain times. After you fail you need to take time to rethink the whole process, and think about a new venture. You keep repeating the process over and over until you break through. You're going to learn a lot. You're going to get closer to your success each time you try.

Through repetition, you'll achieve your goals and start stretching them into bigger dreams. You will be amazed by what you've achieved and will continue to achieve. Just believe in yourself and stay efficient.

When you face tough times and problems, make a list of them. Then make lists of solutions for these problems. Analyze the solutions, select one and go with it. Keep testing and correcting mistakes you've made. This is a journey. Keep absorbing what's going on around you, keep learning and always be strategic about your actions.

Always consider and guard your reputation, because if you lose money, you can always make it back, but if you lose your reputation, it might be lost forever.

Build and Leave a Legacy

A legacy is something that you leave for your kids, your community, for other people, or a certain industry — or country. It's something you leave for the next generation. And for that, they will remember you.

Sometimes you work on your legacy without even realizing what you'll see come to fruition. When U.S. President John F. Kennedy in 1961 presented Americans with his challenge to put a man on the moon and return him safely to Earth by the end of the 1960's, he probably never dreamed of the wonders of science and technology that would emerge from the launch of the space program.

Just like Kennedy, you too can leave a legacy.

There are different types of legacies you can designate. They can be financial — an example is a father who leaves some money for his wife and kids. Or, a person can change the way a certain industry thinks. The perfect example is Steve Jobs, who revolutionized the mobile and computer industry. Thomas Edison helped provide electricity, and afterward General Electric focused on power and energy products.

Some humanitarian legacies have begun to solve problems of disease, cancer, and poverty in Africa. Other examples concern saving certain animal species, such as dolphins.

Many people don't think about legacy at all, which is a huge mistake. You need to be responsible and disciplined enough to leave something behind you for the next generation; the people who survive after your death should remember you for something good you left behind. Your legacy and what you've achieved throughout your life is what you'll be remembered for.

It takes time to build a legacy. Think about it. What's your purpose in this life and what's the value that you can add to others? This might take you years or decades to figure it out, but it's your mission in this life. Maybe it will be a book, a product or service.

Learn the Art of Self Discipline

"With self-discipline most anything is possible."
— Theodore Roosevelt

Self-discipline is one of the major requirements for your success in any path that you take in your business or life. It's the ability to control your emotions so that you can engage in targeted actions to achieve your goals.

The good news is that discipline is a learnable thing. When you work out at the gym, the result is that your muscles and body get stronger. The same thing happens when you improve your state of mind by improving your discipline. It takes practice. It's a way to practice holding yourself accountable for certain projects — to finish a book, start a company, benefit other people in the world.

Discipline is used in the military and in schools. It's used to teach soldiers and students to achieve certain goals. It's a habit you can develop with practice and over time. It's a way of teaching yourself through repetition. Any action you repeat over and over again can become an automatic habit.

There are many tools you can use to improve your level of discipline, such as "to do" lists and calendars. You can also use a vision board – on your desktop, on your wall, with pictures of your dream – to keep yourself motivated. It's best to prioritize your tasks to achieve the most important ones first, so if your day starts in the morning, before checking your emails or doing anything that's going to drain your brain, start instead by doing the most important tasks on your "to do" list. Set the most productive time for you throughout the day, and discipline yourself to that time in your daily goals.

If you want to be a successful investor, you need to be able to control your emotions and be self-disciplined enough to stand firm when you negotiate. You need to learn how to pick the right investments and analyze them properly, and be disciplined enough to stick with your long-term investment plan.

Most successful people are self-disciplined. If you study successful people's bios, you will find them focused through certain practices or techniques to achieve what they want. Unsuccessful people usually don't have plans. They are undisciplined and tend to act on urgent but less important things throughout their lives, so they end up achieving nothing and leaving this life with no mark or achievement to be remembered.

Consider Failure One of Your Greatest Tools

The most valuable thing you can make is a mistake...
you can't learn anything from being perfect."
— Adam Osborne

Most people fear failure, especially when they make the transition to entrepreneur. Still, I want to emphasize, even though I've said it before, that failure is the greatest tool in learning life lessons. When you fail, you learn. After you fail you start thinking, you take a break for a while, then you come back with an adjusted mindset.

If you have a certain project you're working on, try as best as you can to calculate the failure depth, so you know where you're heading as well as the worst-case scenario of damage that could happen.

Sometimes when you look back at what you've done before and the challenges and failures that you've faced, you realize that these occurrences are really what shaped you up to succeed later.

In some of my ventures, I've felt a business at a certain point start declining, and I tried my best to find solutions to buy time to test more methods to try and make the business work; but then I realized at the end that there was no hope to continue based on the tools I had at that point. It's important to remember to apply the lessons from your previous failure project to the new one.

Tip: For more tips about entrepreneurship please visit aktips.com

It's important to not to quit your dream because you have failed before, because the biggest failure is quitting your dream.

CHAPTER 5

THE IMPORTANCE OF YOUR PURPOSE, VISION AND ACTIONS

"The only thing worse than being blind is having sight but no vision."
— Helen Keller

Having a vision is an essential part of going after anything you want to achieve — in your business, your happiness, your life. To find your vision, ask yourself what you want in your life. Then, imagine experiencing a perfect day. What would you do and who would you spend time with? Once you have a vision of a perfect day, extend it to a perfect month and a perfect year. A clear vision is important because it is easy to become overwhelmed by the chaos of life. Your vision can help you decide which opportunities to pursue and what needs to be eliminated.

An entrepreneur creates a vision for putting things together, creating sources for projects and envisioning them in a way that perhaps nobody can see except him or her. Be realistic when you shape your vision and take it step by step; divide it into small goals so you're not overwhelmed. It's important to look ahead and visualize not only the beginning of a project, but also the end. You want to foresee the future and predict it in your own unique way, which is a result of your background, your previous ventures and experiences, as well as your failures and successes.

After working for five years in the corporate world in Dubai, I couldn't tolerate the employment life anymore. The entrepreneurial spirit was calling me from somewhere within. At this point I already had good skills in terms of planning, management, sales and marketing, so I started building my first franchise brand. At the same time, I started attending seminars to see what I could learn. I didn't know the meaning of the word "entrepreneur" back then even though, ironically, Iraq was a very entrepreneurial country, on a small scale, consisting primarily of self-employed people who managed their own shops. I criticized the entrepreneurial style in Iraq because its methods were not systematic. It operated under the "old school" style that lacks any branding or automation. Basically, the customer comes to the shop to ask the owner of the shop to help him/her buy things instead of visiting the shop for its branded products or services.

I believed that I had a newer, better vision for doing business in a new professional and systematic branded way in Iraq. Many challenged me and said that I couldn't do this or that in Iraq, but I did. It's good to keep in mind that our goals and vision shift over time, especially when we travel out of our comfort zone.

The businesses I'm creating these days are more systematic, automated and efficient. I focus mainly on creating those that work without me — franchises, chains, or other types of business that involve delegating authority after they are shaped and empowering employees so they can lead without my direct involvement in the operations. I study and plan a business for delegation before even getting involved in it. I'll never get involved in a business that cannot be done in this way, because I know that nobody will take care of it after a certain point other than me if the business is designed to be dependent on my involvement, consume most of my time and limit the leveragability of the business.

I always plan to eliminate myself from operations, and work mainly *on* the business rather than *in* the business.

When I create a business, I'm involved in shaping the structure and system for three to six months. Then I start delegating. I will review the numbers and start hiring smart people, those who know how to develop the system. I act as a consultant more than a business owner or manager. I focus on adding value through any business or project before thinking about earning money, because if you add real value, the money will follow. Then I think about legacy, leaving my touch on this world with something that helps others.

When a customer asks specifically for you, focus on automating your business and building a brand around your product — not you. The more you learn, the more your vision stretches and expands your goals. There's nothing wrong with growing and changing with the times.

Purpose is the Core

Your purpose is the very deep core of your existence, the reason and drive for why you exist in this world, why you are doing what you are doing, what you want to accomplish with your life and your legacy.

Is your purpose to train, help, advise, heal, nurture, love or create? You act from your purpose when you are fulfilled and adding value to the world. What is that special thing you do that is your greatest contribution to the world? That's your purpose.

Your purpose is your big why, the reason that you do everything you do in life and in your career. Your purpose is continuous, it doesn't stop when you reach a goal.

Once you are clear on your purpose, look at your mission and vision. To successfully achieve your vision and mission, you must be using your life purpose.

When you know your person purpose, consider the purpose of your business. Every successful business has a purpose. For example, Southwest Airlines states that their purpose is to connect people to what is important in their lives through friendly, reliable and low-cost air travel. If you are an entrepreneur, having a clear purpose for each of your businesses will be very helpful.

Vision Is the Where

"Logic will get you from A to B. Imagination will take you everywhere."
— Albert Einstein

A vision tells you where you want to go or how you want the world to see you or your business. You may strive to be the world's best, or a market leader, or a philanthropist who supports schools in impoverished areas. Your vision for your company may include winning awards for innovation, breaking the million-dollar sales mark, or having your brand become a household name.

To develop your vision, find books that deal with expanding your horizon. Network with people who've achieved the success that you can't yet visualize so they can help you expand your horizon. They can see things that you can't see yet. If you want to be a successful author or speaker, network with authors and speakers. If you want to be an entrepreneur, attend entrepreneurial seminars or register for an incubator or co-working space for startups.

Visualize how your life is going to be three, five or ten years from now. What's the big picture of your business or life? You need to keep looking until you're able to define your purpose. Once your purpose is uncovered, a vision is likely to arise. You can use techniques to help you achieve this. For example, you can create a vision board.

Put your dream in front of you wherever you go, so your subconscious mind keeps thinking about it. Practice thinking about your dream and seeing it wherever you go. Start small, think big, and then start taking action. Divide your dream into small goals and work on them one-by-one.

Ask yourself when you want to retire. Does retirement sound exciting to you because it works for some and kills others? How much money do you want to make? What are your business goals? Do you want to have a family? You need to sit and picture how you want your life to be. The more you learn, the more you personally change and then modify your vision.

As you create it, think deeply about what you really want, and write everything down. Put it on paper where you can see it. Share it with people, and get their opinions. I've said it before, and I say it again: Always listen to your inner voice, believe in what you want to achieve, and then be persistent in achieving it. It's not wrong to look at the vision of people who are more successful than you; from them you can learn things that you can't see at your current mindset level.

Mission Is the How

Your mission is the how question—how you will accomplish your vision. A mission sets the direction and focus of your company, it shapes your strategy and processes. When you write your mission, statement include a summary of competencies and competitive differentiations. For example, I'm or my x company is the world's best -----, will provide you with the best -----, with unique capabilities and uniqueness in ----- to add the best value to my clients.

Create a personal mission as well as a business mission statement to guide your actions and keep you on track.

Values Are More Important Than You Think

Your values are the glue that holds everything together, your decisions, relationships, processes, and investments. Core values are the principles, attitudes and emotions that you will not compromise. Examples of values include things like:

- Integrity
- Diversity
- Profitability
- Innovation
- Kindness
- Honesty
- Efficiency
- Respect

Be clear about identifying and listing your values or company's values. Because values drive behavior, they are vitally important for personal and corporate success.

Your purpose and values should not change. They are the core of your identity or the identity of your business. Your vision and mission will evolve over time. Each success gives you the opportunity to expand your vision and mission to achieve more and work in a more efficient way.

Passion Is Temporary

You may have heard the phrase—follow your passion. I disagree with this advice. Passions change with time. You may be passionate about skiing today but find that passion fades when you break your leg. Your passions include your hobbies and interests, things that you do for enjoyment as well as in your career.

Your passion is all about you; it may even feel a bit selfish. Passion is a strong and barely controllable emotion. To identify your passions, think of all the things you enjoy in life. Then, narrow your focus until you have identified the things you love so much that you can't imagine not doing ever again. Your passions will call you over and over during your life. Some of my passions include sports, personal development, learning, and efficiency.

A life well lived includes many passions. However, when you are clear on your purpose in life, your passions will be focused on achieving that purpose. Your purpose remains with you throughout your life. It keeps you awake at night because you care about it so much, and is the thing you most want to share with the world to make it a better place.

The Difference Between Goals and Vision

A goal is not a vision. A goal ends by achieving something, while a vision remains open-ended.

For example, you can set a goal of writing a book, and your goal ends by writing it. But if your vision is to be an author, you can write many books, and your reputation as an author will never end.

If your goal is to open a restaurant, then this goal will end when you open one. If your vision is to be an entrepreneur for the rest of your life, you may open many different businesses and you will still be called an entrepreneur.

Your goal is part of your vision; your vision may include a series of goals. You set the vision first, which is the big picture, and then set goals to get closer to achieving this vision and fulfilling it, step by step, goal by goal.

A vision is more subjective, while a goal tends to be more objective. You can measure a goal. A vision is ongoing. It's about the long path to your destination. With each step, you see the next step more clearly.

Martin Luther King Jr. in his famous "I Have a Dream" speech imagined a world different from the one he was in. He said, "I have a dream that my four little children will one day live in a nation where they will not be judged by the color of their skin but by the content of their character." He also said, "I have a dream that one day on the red hills of Georgia, the sons of former slaves and the sons of former slave owners will be able to sit down together at the table of brotherhood." Dr. King's vision is still alive and will go on guiding people long after his death.

President John F. Kennedy announced the Apollo Moon Project, whose goal was to put a man on the moon by the end of 1960s. The purpose of the goal was to win the space race, but his vision of going beyond our wildest dreams lives on.

Losing 10 kilograms (22 pounds) is a goal; staying healthy is a vision. Getting out of debt is a goal; being financially free is a vision. Running your own company is a goal; becoming an entrepreneur is a vision.

How to Set Goals

Learning how to set goals is one of the most important steps in the success of your life. It's difficult to have a roadmap for your life, or accomplish a vision, without setting goals. Some may be personal goals, such as wanting to achieve success within your family, wanting to change your attitude, or lose weight as part of your health goals.

Sometimes we have happiness goals, such as planning a vacation, taking a dance class, jumping out of a plane for an adrenaline rush — going after anything we consider a fun adventure.

Some of us have social or relationships goals; others have educational goals — to change their mindset, for example. And still others have career and financial goals, which include achieving success as an entrepreneur or employee.

It's normal to experience a certain shift in your goals every few years, but you need to direct your shift toward something positive that will add more depth to your life.

Perhaps you'll have a goal that contributes to society, a desire to achieve something, solve a problem, or contribute to scientific research that will serve millions of people, or resolve a poverty issue.

Next to my desk at home, I have a small white board. Sometimes I write on it the things I want to do daily, such as a blog post or complete a part of this book. The things I write on this small white board are what I want to include as a daily habit. An entry might be: writing 500 words of my book, playing squash or going to a Yoga class, creating an interview for my web TV show "Be Efficient TV."

In front of each goal, write what methods you plan to achieve that goal. You might write down 100 of them and then select the ones you consider top priority, and the best ways to accomplish them. Then, start implementing them. There are long-term goals such as those related to your career. Those need to be divided into shorter goals to be achieved, which will make the process easier for you to digest. Long-term goals should be divided into several missions or chapters to be achieved within certain deadlines.

Another thing I do is set yearly goals. Every December I write my goals for the next year and review them every one to two weeks to check my progress. If the goals are small tasks, I tend to make them recurring reminders on my iPhone calendar, like two blog posts set to reoccur on two different days during the week, or schedule 20 social media posts through buffer once a week, or contact the leasing department of five malls once a week. Sometimes I schedule a certain recurring task on a daily basis. While it may be only one task that can be done in five minutes, there could be something annoying about that task that keeps me procrastinating and not doing it, so I schedule it daily in my calendar until I do it. Then I remove it from my calendar. The point is that sometimes you need to trick your mind or force it to abide by certain methods to deliver certain results.

This task-scheduling exercise can work on anything you want to achieve in your life or business. The point is to create consistent focused action that turns into automatic habit that will help you get closer to your annual goals and achieve your long-term vision.

You start with one — one by one — and keep reviewing and correcting your steps to achieve whatever you want to achieve. Understand what benefits these goals will provide. Why are these goals important to you? How exactly are you going to achieve them?

Put a deadline on a goal, even if you don't meet it. When you have one, you feel pressure to act. Even if you don't meet the deadline, which might make you feel guilty, this might inspire you to take more focused action to achieve your goal as soon as possible. You can always revise the deadline.

The most important step, once you've listed your goals, is to take action. So many people have dreams, but don't act to achieve them.

Compare the pain of not achieving a goal with the pleasure you'll get after you achieve one. Always set a goal higher than what you want to achieve to expand your horizon. But be realistic! If you are currently reaching $10,000 in monthly sales and want to achieve $12,000, aim for $15,000. If you make your target $12,000, you'll likely achieve between $10,000 and $12,000 because your subconscious mind may not push you more than that.

> *"Vision without action is daydreaming,*
> *and action without vision is a nightmare."*
> — Chinese Proverb

Strategy Is Composed of Tactics

Just as your vision has a greater meaning than your goal, the same distinction can be applied to strategy and tactics. You need to create a number of tactics to implement a strategy. The purpose of creating a strategy is to define and deliver goals, while the purpose of tactics is to use resources or techniques to execute smaller goals to achieve your strategy.

Strategy is more long-term and represents an overall picture for what you want to achieve, in a business, an organization, a war or in your life. Tactics are the actions that will help you make your thoughts a reality.

An example of strategy is a personal one that Olympic swimmer Michael Phelps learned from a coach. Going after his 10th gold medal of his career, while he was in the race, his goggles filled with water and he couldn't see anything. He kept swimming and nevertheless broke the world record. His strategy came from a habit he performs before any race. He closes his eyes and envisions the race, stroke by stroke, from start to finish. He pictures himself using perfect strokes and seeing exactly how many strokes he'll need to get from start to finish. He plays a mental video of what he envisions as the perfect race. When the time came to compete, he had already run the race in his mind and envisioned how perfect that race would feel.

You can apply this strategy to anything you do. When you have a clear vision of where you want to go and can envision your path from within, your focus will help you reach your goals and, in some way, win your own gold medal.

The concepts of strategy and tactics are most often associated with wars and military stories from the past, such as what we read in *The Art of War*,[4] by Sun Tzu, a Chinese military general, or what we

---

[4]   Tzu, Sun. *The Art of War*. Originally published 513 BC. XX: Oxford, United Kingdom: Oxford University Press, 1963.

have learned from recent military generals' books, or politicians such as Franklin Delano Roosevelt or Winston Churchill. There's also what we learn from Robert Greene books such as *The 48 Laws of Power*,[5] *The 33 Strategies of War*,[6] or *The 50th Law*,[7] a book he wrote with 50 Cent which I consider the most realistic about life and business. The latter discusses how difficult life and business can be and how we need to look at our failure in order to overcome it. Still, we can create strategy and tactics for more positive reasons.

Vision: to be financially free within five years.

Goal: to generate passive income of $20,000 per month.

Strategy: to achieve the goal by building a franchise business that will generate passive income through royalties.

Tactics: to have a specific design for the franchise concept, a feel for the brand, an online and offline marketing plan and a detailed operating manual.

A great strategy does not depend on brilliant tactics for success. If the idea is strong enough, you don't need complicated tactics. To be efficient, simplify your business concepts so you require fewer tactics to achieve success.

These days, both business and life are becoming more competitive with time, so you need to be strategic more often than you have been to achieve your life and business goals. Remember to look at and evaluate your results more often than you used to.

Don't be concerned about losing some battles.
What you want is to win the war.

---

[5] Greene, Robert. *The 48 Laws of Power*. London: Viking Penguin, 2000.

[6] Greene, Robert. *The 33 Strategies of War*. London: Viking Penguin, 2006.

[7] Green, Robert & 50 Cent. *The 50th Law*. NY: HarperCollins, 2009.

Sharing Your Idea Brings It to Life

Recently, I was sitting at a café with a friend discussing some business ideas. My friend began to tell me about an idea he had. At first, he was hesitant to say anything about it, because although it was not crowded at the café, there were some people sitting around us. Finally, my friend decided he would go ahead and share the idea with me. As he was talking, he kept turning his head to make sure no one was listening. He kept repeating that he wanted this idea to stay between the two of us.

In this situation, this was someone with a great business idea, who never takes action. As a result, the idea dies. The key to succeeding is to make sure that, if you have an idea for a business, you take the next step and implement it. Talking is good, but not enough. Far too often, people have an idea for a business and see that someone else has implemented the same idea. The difference is that one person acted on an idea and the other person did not. Don't allow yourself to fall into this trap. There is no need to try to reinvent the wheel.

Facebook, as we all know, is wildly successful. Even so, it was hardly the first social media site. Long before Facebook, there was MySpace. After Facebook, there was Instagram. Both sites have enjoyed great success. They are both built on the same basic social media idea.

There's no need to be afraid to share your idea. If you do not act and share your idea with investors and others, nothing will come of it. There are many great services out there available for consulting that can help you get your business off the ground — for example, Clarity. fm. With this service, you can chat with experts from a wide variety of different fields. You are charged per minute, but it is a valuable service. You can also begin to attend startup events for entrepreneurs where you can network with others. Another option is to take advantage of the Internet. The Internet has significantly changed the way we communicate. You can find practically anything you want at the speed of light, through such sites as Google and YouTube.

Many people never act to implement their ideas. As a result, they never realize anything from their idea. Bring your idea to light. Don't be afraid to share your idea because you may have to share profits with certain partners. Bring your idea to light and share your success with others. Don't be afraid that someone else will steal your idea. This happens rarely. You can have people sign a non-disclosure agreement (NDA) before you discuss your idea with them, but be aware that investors may ignore your idea if you do this.

In the end, the key is not the idea itself. Whoever is willing to implement it is what affects the success of any venture. Be willing to take action, share your idea, and embrace success.

Believe Your Inner Voice

"Your time is limited, so don't waste it living someone else's life. Don't be trapped by dogma, which is living with the results of other people's thinking. Don't let the noise of others' opinions drown out your own inner voice. And most important, have the courage to follow your heart and intuition."
— Steve Jobs

Sometimes, regardless of all your calculations, studies and plans, your inner voice tells you something different from scientific studies or such logical forces as your family, friends, or environment. Most great entrepreneurs who've uncovered a new idea usually began with people laughing at them – people who told them that their project would never work.

At first, Mark Zuckerberg did not believe that Facebook would compare with MySpace. He questioned the two men who came up with the concept of Facebook about how it would compare. But step-by-step, it became a mega success, becoming an Internet company with the highest stock value in the technology industry. At one point, people questioned if the evaluation of the company was real since, when it decided to go public, it was valued more than McDonald's.

To break through, you must believe in your inner voice. If Mark Zuckerberg had come to you and asked you to invest $10,000 in a project he had called Facebook, you likely would have told him he was crazy. But if you had done it, your $10,000 would now be worth a number with many zeros.

To achieve what you want, it's essential to believe in yourself and to listen to your inner voice.

Practice trusting yourself. Even if your inner voice is not mature enough to be right most of the time, you will learn. You will make mistakes and be persistent enough to correct them. Once you've accomplished this, you will trust yourself even more. Listening to your inner voice doesn't mean that you don't have to consult with other people. Consulting with others can provide you with a variety of ideas. You consult with mentors, read books, do research, but what differentiates you is how you put the information together and create output from it in your own way. This is what makes you unique.

Everybody has a different point of view, a distinct way of working. Sports competitors are differentiated by their individual techniques, tactics and achievements. Companies are distinguished by their numbers, branding, or the quality of their product.

I have failed at many projects. When you fail, people around you may blame you or attempt to show that you're irresponsible and made mistakes. This is human nature. Rather than accept a mistake as an opportunity to learn, some people choose to blame. It's possible that they are scared or don't believe you can accomplish your dream. When you fail, they are the first to say, "I told you but you didn't listen to me." When you succeed, they will act proud that you've done it.

Even people who are happy for your success sometimes will blame you when you fail. They don't encourage you to try again. They try to point out the issues — you've been irresponsible, you rushed into things, you need to alter your character. At times like this, you might need time for yourself, time to think — perhaps in a coffee shop, or go for a walk in a park, or stay home and contemplate the situation.

Life sends you signals all the time, sometimes via an action by somebody around you, in a movie scene, in a speech you hear. When that kind of signal clicks in your mind, it's only for you; only you can translate it, believe it, and take action based on your belief, knowledge and experience to achieve your goal that gets you closer to your vision. The more you push yourself out of your comfort zone, the more you strengthen your knowledge and experience. The more knowledge and experience you gain, the wiser your actions become.

The Power of Focus and Direction

Due to huge technological development in the world today, we're surrounded by such devices as small laptops, smartphones, PlayStation portables, and pads — all of which keep us connected with social media, email and other time-consuming items. These inventions have been designed to save us time, but in fact they make us busier and less focused.

Most of us are continually connected to the Internet or to a gaming gadget that puts us in an anti-focus state of mind. We spend so much time entertaining ourselves, posting photos about our life or responding to urgent emails that we ignore what's really important. Hours, days, months, years, and decades pass quickly with less action in the long run on important things. People spend their lives watching TV and scrolling their Facebook pages to look at other successful people instead of acting to change their own current stage of life.

I stopped writing for weeks and sometimes months to take care of urgent business details and left my book behind. Completing my book isn't urgent but it's important long-term. My book is a legacy of personal thoughts and ideas that might add value to other people's lives and hopefully will make people remember me for something that helped them in this world.

The solution for us all to achieve something meaningful is to focus, and to develop the habit of doing what's most important first thing in the morning, first thing after taking a shower, or first thing after watching a movie during a needed break. If you spend your entire day checking emails, you'll be left with no brain power to act on what's most vital. When you've structured your day, your week will be fixed. Once you fix your week, your month will be organized, and so on until you plan your entire life and achieve what you want.

Some of us know better than others how to use our time wisely. There are constant, ongoing distractions in this life. It's up to you to focus on what's going to get you where you want to go.

There are dozens of software programs that can calculate your productivity, by viewing sites where you spend time. There's software called Rescue Time (https://www.rescuetime.com), a personal analytics service that calculates how you spend your time and offers tools to help you be more productive. I use also Anti-Social (https://anti-social.cc) to block specific social media platforms for a specific period of time so I can focus on immediate, important things. I use Freedom (https://anti-social.cc) to block the Internet and websites completely for a specific period of time. I create a "to do" list and "not to do list" which are helpful focus techniques. Learning how to say "no" is another powerful technique.

You can use Stephen Covey's Time Management Grid, which appears in *First Things First.*[8] Like Robert Kiyosaki, Covey makes use of four quadrants. His are: Important and Urgent, Important and Not Urgent, Not Important and Urgent, Not Important and Not Urgent.

---

[8] Covey, Stephen, A. Roger Merrill, Rebecca R. Merrill. *First Things First: To Live, Love, to Learn, to Leave a Legacy.* NY: Simon & Schuster, 1994.

The First Quadrant (Urgent & Important)

This quadrant is about necessary activities:

- Crises
- Deadline-driven activities
- Medical emergencies
- Other "true" emergencies
- Pressing problems
- Last minute preparations

The key action word for this quadrant is "manage" as these important and urgent activities are required, as is extreme care to manage and take care of them.

The Second Quadrant (Important & Not Urgent)

This quadrant is about the quality and personal leadership activities:

- Preparation and planning
- Values clarification
- Empowerment
- Relationship-building
- True recreation

The key action word for this quadrant is "focus." These are the activities at which highly successful people excel and less successful people fail. Since these activities are important but not urgent, there's no time pressure to achieve them. This is why most people ignore these activities and, as a result, miss achievements in their lives. These activities are your greatest mission and part of your legacy.

I also use my small white board that I keep next to my desk or sofa where I work or my iPhone calendar, and write the major three to five not-urgent but important tasks I must achieve every day, and tick them off the list throughout the day. These tasks make me feel happy when they're achieved. They boost my self-satisfaction and energy level and inspire me to achieve more throughout the day.

The Third Quadrant (Not Important & Urgent)

This quadrant is described by the word "deception" because the activities of this quadrant can be misleading:

- Meeting other people's priorities and expectations
- Frequent interruptions
- Most emails, some calls
- Urgency masquerading as importance

The key action words for this quadrant are "use caution" or "avoid." This quadrant teaches us that we need to learn to say "no" more often, or delegate others to act on certain activities. Outsourcing is great for delegating non-important activities.

The Fourth Quadrant (Not Important & Not Urgent)

This quadrant is described by the word "waste" because the activities of this quadrant are a complete waste of our time.

- Escapist activities
- Mindless television-watching
- Busywork
- Junk mail
- Some emails
- Some calls

The key action word for this quadrant is "avoid." We need to learn to say a big fat "No!" more often, and learn to take control of our life by avoiding these bad habits and replacing them with more productive ones.

When I do something that I feel is important, let's say writing a certain section of my book first thing in the morning, or finish a project that's been delayed, the action gives me a boost through the day and removes the regret factor I feel when I'm overwhelmed by urgent responsibilities.

When you take care of important activities at the beginning of your productivity session, no matter what time of day, you'll feel better about everything else. You need to always give everything its proper time and divide your time well — time to spend with friends, family, on anything important and/or urgent. And you need to delegate as much as you can.

Creating too many new projects at one time will drain your focus, but the more team members you have, the more you can delegate and focus on priorities. If you feel it might be distracting to create a new project or develop a new idea, put it on your "to do" list of future projects and prioritize until you get the right people, resources and time to act on them.

When you see the success of other people and are inspired by them, it's a good time to take action. Most of us are motivated when we see successful people, but don't always consider what those successful people do to get to where they are. We attend seminars by these people, get inspired and wowed, and then when we go back to normal life, we get back into our routine, our comfort zone, our rat race.

Finding the right information and tools when you need them is essential to enhance your level of focus. I use iMindMap (https://app. imindmap.com) to draw mind maps for some projects or presentations. It draws up a plan for you, with steps and directions to achieve more within very limited time. I use the program 2Do (www.2doapp.com) on my iPhone and Mac, or a "To Do" list on Evernote. You can also use a file cabinet to organize your documents in your office or home. These productivity tools and techniques help you get things done.

When people see my pages on Facebook and the projects I'm working on, they ask, "How are you doing all of that?" Some friends or associates, when they come to my city, don't contact me because they think I'm busy. I am busy, but I'm efficient and delegate most of the mechanics and repeated work, so I can focus only on what I consider most important. Sometimes, I have more than 10 virtual assistants working with me. I can meet anybody anytime I want. I can work when I want from wherever I want.

I have a social media person who gives me a plan a month in advance to approve. Once I approve it, he schedules the posts and does the work. I trained these helpers to do what's needed. After a while, they do these things better than I ever could. This is the idea, to train people to do things better so you can focus on priorities and achieve more things in less time.

Life keeps pushing us out of our focus zone. We must fight back and learn to develop habits that allow us to take control of our lives, step by step, habit by habit, till we take maximum control and learn to focus on what we want to achieve in order to leave this world a better place than we found it.

Time Is Your Most Precious Asset

"If you want to make good use of your time, you've got to know what's most important and then give it all you've got."
— Lee Iacocca

Sooner or later we're all going to die, and time is the most precious thing we have. With time, we can create a life, value, experiences, money or anything else we want. Spend your time with the right people; spend it with the people you love. Spend it with people who will help and support you, people who care about you, people who will take you to the next level, lift you up, and teach you something to enrich your life and help you add value to this universe. Read books, educate yourself, and pursue your dreams. Stop wasting time and living the life other people want you to live. Live the life you want, the one you've been dreaming about.

The time that's passing now will never come back. Spend your time on experiences more than things. Spend your time on learning, on pursuing happiness, fulfillment and legacy rather than money. You will not be remembered for your money and you will not take your money with you. You will be remembered for the value you've added during your life — that's your legacy. These are the only things that will stand out when you die, the things that will become your legacy.

Many people spend their lives battling for authority, for positions, chairs, money, power — and most of them live and die without knowing why they are here or their real purpose in this life.

It's important to think about why you're here, how you will leave a mark on this universe, your mission in this life, how you want to live it, what you want to do in it, with whom you want to spend it, and how you want to be remembered.

Every passing minute is irreversible; when it's gone, it's gone. With every day, you have less time.

If you can just pause for only one minute a day, think about what you want to achieve, break your life into years, your years into months, your months into days, and your days into seconds and think of how you want to spend this time. Regardless of how little time you have, you can still have a great impact on the people around you, and on the world, if you use it wisely.

Learn to develop the right habits and eliminate bad habits from your life so you can save time and use it wisely with a better outcome, better legacy. Every second is a precious gift.

Be Yourself and Focus on What You Do Best

> *"The future belongs to those who learn more skills and*
> *combine them in creative ways."*
> — Robert Greene

I'm not saying that everything popular is always wrong, or that you shouldn't follow the crowd in any activity practiced by many people. I don't mean that if there's a certain popular product used by many people, this means that it's not a good product. But one of the examples of the wrong-crowd theory is the percentage of employees in the total working force in the world. It's higher than 90%. The percentage of wealthy employees is less than 10% and most of this 10% still don't enjoy the freedom of their time the way they'd like, because their mindset is structured to work in the same way as all employees, even though they may work at a higher level or better position.

This is similar to the 80/20 law, which states that 20% of the people own 80% of the money, and 80% of people own 20% of the money. Joseph Juran,[9] while working for the government in Washington, D.C. during World War II, came across the work of Vilfredo Pareto and named the 19th century Italian professor of political economy's "80/20 rule" — that the top 20% of any country's population accounts for more or less 80% of its total income. The assumption is that most results in any situation are determined by a small number of causes.

We are always affected by our environment. Our parents most often want us to be like their generation's doctors or engineers because they think this is the best path for us to take. They tend to ignore all the natural forces related to our passions. Their parents advised them to study hard, get good grades, and go to a good university in order to get a high paying job, and that's what they pass down to us. The structure of our economy is designed to continue in this way.

If you don't have a plan, you're not going to get anywhere. It's like traveling to a new country without a map.

Leaders usually go places where nobody has been before. Let people follow you. If you want to be a leader, start leading now. Pull together the people you're leading and start leading them. You need to

---

[9] *The Economist*, June 19, 2009

be the director of the movie of your life. You need to distinguish yourself from others and develop your own persona so people recognize you. Be unique, be innovative, be yourself, and focus on what you do best.

Many people like to spend their life watching the game. I like to be in the game. When I quit my last job, I remember that I was partially managing my father's business online and overseas for a very small commission that I knew would not lead me anywhere and was mainly focused on the learning experience and adding value to my father's company. While quitting my job may not have been a wise decision at the time, I felt I had had enough, was glad I'd done it, but could not take it anymore.

I'm not saying you should quit your job, but sometimes you need to follow your inner voice and take risks to stretch yourself; otherwise you'll stay limited trying to climb the employment career ladder, fearing the thought of taking any new action, especially with the pressure of increasing expenses.

When I talk to colleagues with whom I went to school or worked together in the corporate world, most still don't know what to do other than secure their current chair or look for a better paying job.

Escaping the employment rat race is not about the next great idea, as an idea is no more than 5% to 10 % of a project. Taking massive action towards your idea is what makes it matter in the market — to gain attraction, momentum and market share that creates the boom. Regardless of how many courses you take, how many books you read, you have to take action. Learning by doing is the best way.

Real experience gives you a different kind of exposure, because usually you're doing a something you've never done before. That's why I advise the hiring of a mentor who's done it and been through what you're trying to do. A mentor can guide you on your path. Experience will help you learn from challenges you'll face. A mentor is not necessarily someone better than you at what you do, but rather someone who knows how to bring out the best in you. The best example is any successful sport coach who is never necessarily a better player than the player he's coaching.

You're going to learn from people with whom you spend most of your time, so change the people around you if you want to change your life. Understand that you are the average of the five people you associate yourself with.

When you start a new venture, calculate the worst-case scenario as best you can, and how much you might lose, so you can plan on how to survive. Your calculations should enable you to survive at least six to twelve months.

When I open one of my businesses in a new city or country, I study things. The first study I engage in is usually the least perfect one. After I open another branch, if it's in the same city, that plan is going to be more precise than the previous project in the same city.

Take action! If you aren't sure how to begin, try to partner with other people who have an idea, or read books about start-ups, goals and vision. The more you read, the more ideas you get, the more you act, the more you find the right mentors, partners, and team members.

The real world isn't always right. It's necessary to realize that what you see around you might not be what's right for you.

Your first time out is the riskiest, as you lack real control and rightfully feel that you're standing on shaky ground. This feeling affects your character, decisions and principles as you have to offer what you believe in order to guard your future. It's best to begin small and get some experience; then you can move on to more challenging paths.

The solution is to plan for your next project or idea even if you keep your job for the next five years. Start now to work on something that can create more passive income for you and your family. Then, when you stop working, you have something to cover your expenses.

My advice is to live in one, two, even five, years of entrepreneurial fear until you break through into the life you want. Dedicate one or two hours of your day to working on or planning something new as your first entrepreneurial step. Writing this book has not been an easy task, but I have allocated one to two hours a day to write a goal of one to three pages. With this small target, I've been able to finish the book. This is my first book so it's taken me two years since I was not consistent about my writing. For a couple of months, I was testing and discovering new methods of writing and structuring the book. My next book will be written in a much shorter period of time. Sometimes we need to jump into something and struggle through the process until we find the best system that works for us.

Don't follow the crowd. The world around you isn't always right. The real world is all about people going to their jobs thinking that there is no other way to make money or to live their lives financially free.

People nowadays spend their lives watching and analyzing sports or politics, even if they're not taking any part in them. I think being in the picture or performing the action is better than watching the action. You make the news instead of observing it.

Remove TV and cable service from your life. Go to YouTube and watch whatever you like. Go to iTunes and buy whatever you like, instead of waiting two hours, flipping channels waiting for your best or favorite program to start, and fast forwarding through commercials. This will save you time and you'll feel much happier. Stop watching the news; it's not going to change your life.

So, don't follow the crowd. If you want to make money, consult with some mentors about money, with people who make money. If you want to be happy, ask happy people how they do it. Not all successful people are happy. If you want to be physically fit, work with a personal trainer — someone who knows how to achieve fitness.

Desire is an essential factor in deciding where to head next. You need to ask yourself repeatedly whether that thing you are planning to do is right for you or not. Don't try to live others' people lives. Be yourself and follow your passion. If you don't, you'll get bored, and quit.

If you want to make money, then you need a strong desire to make it and to overcome challenges, criticism you'll face from your family and friends, and laughter from those who believe you'll fail.

What you need to see is positive achievement, positive numbers, regardless of whether you enjoy your business or not. Many books focus on doing something you love. For me, it's not always the right advice unless I am operationally involved. The best is to simply do something that works and use automation and delegation techniques if you don't enjoy doing those things.

When I create a project, I care about whether that project is going to add value to certain people. If so, then whether I'm passionate about it or not, I might get in if I can get positive terms of investment and other resources, such as the right team.

Over time, you build experience and get to know that you're right or not from feedback you get. Sometimes you must jump into certain projects to test your inner voice and vision, and that's something I enjoy. Over time, you'll get better and better at the game and discover where your passion is leading you.

Desire is all about you hoping to achieve a certain outcome from your journey. Keep motivating yourself to try different journeys until you figure out which ones you enjoy the most. Then you can focus on those.

Persistence Is What Drives You Forward

"Big shots are only little shots who keep shooting."
— Christopher Morley

In achieving any success I've had, persistence has played an essential role in shaping and completing those successes. Without being persistent, there's no way to meet your goals.

Not quitting on your dreams and being persistent enough is also a skill. Sometimes you're born with it and sometimes you develop it yourself with experience, understanding of what you want to achieve, and how important it is to you.

Never quit your dreams. Never give up unless you've tested and received feedback that your idea will not work based on facts or figures.

I used to feel unlucky and that problems were arising everywhere; that feeling was making me feel negative all the time. Nowadays I train my mind to handle whatever I face as part of the learning game, and I look at it all as an opportunity to learn. Instead of thinking negatively, like Michael Phelps I program my mind as much as I can to see and imagine the positive outcome of what I'm facing, and stay persistent so I can overcome the challenge I'm facing.

Sticking with Your Ethics

Overcoming the challenge does not mean that you always succeed; sometimes you just fight to finish without downgrading your other values.

An example is failing with a project and your partners because of the financial loss. As a result, they sell their principles, don't commit to the agreements they made, and are ready to end their relationship with you for the sake of money. That has happened to me with many projects. For me, failing financially on a project, without losing my principles, is a success because money can be made again, but credibility is difficult to rebuild. You need to think about your commercial benefits in business, but before that you must think about your ethics.

It's human nature to remember losses and complain about them, but most of the time we forget to be thankful for our successes or for whatever we currently have. Remember to be thankful for what's going right for you now, as well as for what's not going the way you want it.

If you are persistent enough to knock on many doors and survive rejection from many different investors or customers, then you'll learn how to keep modifying your products or services until they eventually work. The reason we often see more money earned by people in their 40s rather than in their 20s is because they became wiser with time, with their choices and actions. In today's Information Age, we see people under age 15 or 20 making money, but that doesn't mean they're qualified or experienced enough to hang on to this money. Keeping money is harder than making it.

Rejection is a good teacher for those who've developed an open mindset; staying open to new thoughts and actions is part of the learning game. When a banker rejects your loan application, you will know what to change or do before you apply again at the same bank, or another. Sometimes I contact bank call centers just to learn their requirements for a credit card or a loan. Sometimes I apply to see if they will reject me, and why, so I can modify my approach the next time. Banks are system-based, so you need to understand how to play by their rules.

When I ask friends, getting started with a new idea for a small business, why they don't apply for a credit card to finance the project, many mention that they've tried and were rejected. I tell them that they're not persistent enough; one needs to try more than once. When you are determined and tireless, you not only achieve your goal, but also make people around you believe in who you are and what you're doing, because they see that you don't quit.

**Nobody will believe in you unless
you believe in yourself.**

Maximize Your Happiness and Fulfillment

"To me, success isn't defined by your wallet. It's defined by waking up with a smile on your face, knowing it's going to be a great day. But, sure, money can make your life a whole lot easier."
— *Mark Cuban*

The entrepreneurial road can be tough — and lonely. When things go wrong, especially at the beginning when you're not financially and/ or skillfully solid and lack credibility, you'll find that you're pretty much on your own. You'll see dark and sleepless nights; few people will want to listen to you. However, when you succeed and things are going well, you'll find yourself suddenly barraged by people trying to help, more investors will want to jump in to support you, and more people will attempt to share in your success.

Hang out with entrepreneurs. They will share the pain they've gone through, because they've been there before. They will tell you that what you're going through is normal, and that your sleepless nights will pay off later — if you keep trying. Being persistent is the name of the game.

Success Is Knowing It's Going to Be a Great Day

Many people believe that happiness is the ultimate goal and that it will lead you to success. Others believe that success is the ultimate goal and it will lead you to happiness.

In the world of business, success means achieving a certain outcome or goal within a certain period of time. It can be an attempt to make a certain amount of money, construct a certain building at a certain location, or finish your medical degree to become a doctor. Usually the point of success is to attain a certain amount of wealth, position or honor for a specific performance or achievement.

Most people think that success is what's going to bring us happiness. In fact, success is not a recipe for happiness; it does not create happiness. Success can come from being able to purchase a fancy car; happiness is being able to take a great ride in that car.

Success depends on what it means to you. For some people, success means being a world champion in sports; for others, it means becoming a best-selling author; and for many, it simply means making a lot of money.

Success in business is measured by profit; successful weight loss is measured by the number of kilos or pounds you lose. True success is measured by achieving fulfillment, whether due to great numbers, validation or recognition.

Happiness Comes from a Well-Balanced Life

Happiness is defined by moments of joy. It's a mental or emotional state of wellbeing characterized by positive or pleasant emotions during certain times of our lives.

People generally link happiness with physical and materialistic things, or with achieving certain goals. We often think we're going to be happy after we earn a certain amount of money, graduate from a certain university or buy a specific car. But once we reach what we thought was going to make us happy, we often don't feel it. Also, we sometimes feel miserable about the process of trying to get there.

You cannot find happiness by making it your goal. Happiness is the unintended benefit of pursuing personal dreams and living true to yourself. Happiness is something you choose instead of living your life as if it were a dramatic tragedy, based on struggles you endure on daily basis. Happiness is a choice only you can make in your life. Statistics show that happy and positive people are more successful than negative and unhappy people. While seeking happiness should not be your ultimate goal, wanting to be happy isn't wrong. The happier you are, the better and healthier you will feel and be.

We all know what it's like to feel happy, but have you ever felt truly fulfilled? True happiness comes from a well-balanced life. The freedom to do what we want is essential for happiness.

Success is doing what you love;
happiness is loving what you do.

Fulfillment Comes from Knowing Who You Are

Fulfillment is a state of being in the "flow state" or "being in the zone" and can come with happy experiences or unhappy experiences. You might experience a sad situation but still feel fulfilled. Fulfillment adds richness and depth to your life. It's a long-term way of thinking, found in situations that will last – if not in the physical world, in your memory. Living a life of fulfillment is living true to your values.

In my interview with peak performance coach Arman Sadeghi on my TV show "Be Efficient TV," he mentioned ten different areas we need to focus on and measure to feel fulfillment:

- Family
- Fun and Enjoyment
- Physical Wealth
- Spiritual Wealth
- Emotional Wealth
- Financial Wealth
- Intimacy and Romance
- Career, Mission and Purpose
- Contribution and Giving Back
- Consistent Growth

Define for yourself what you want in each of these areas of life. Write down your purpose, core values, vision, mission and passions for each one. This will help you shape and build your identity, character, values, beliefs and passions. Fulfillment is all about defining your character to add a unique depth and richness to your life.

Important questions to ask yourself if you are lost in life or living an unfulfilled life:

- Am I living a life that's truly meaningful to me?
- Am I doing the best I can with my available energy, resources and resourcefulness?
- Am I leaving a positive impact on the world or the people around me beyond my own joy?

In our interview, Arman Sadeghi told me he had made good money when he was 16 years old. He had a nice flat and car but was still feeling miserable. Some people have a dream of making a million dollars and feel miserable, both on their journey and after they have reached their goal of one million dollars. This is because they were looking for something outside of themselves to make them happy. The reality is that happiness and fulfillment come from within, by defining who you are, what you want and why you want what you want. If you are not happy with who you are and what you have today, then you will never be happy, no matter how many more steps you take.

Happiness is a state of mind.
Fulfillment is a state of being.

Maybe someone close to you is going through terminal cancer that will end in death and you spend the last days and months of that person's life with him or her, making this purpose your main priority. This will bring you sadness but may also add dimension, richness and satisfaction to your life. Seeking fulfillment means you will not only experience happiness but also the rich experience of other emotions, both good and not so good.

Get to know your true identity and the shape of your own character. You don't need a million dollars in the bank to feel like a millionaire. If you have a clear plan for the future, how you're going to make the million dollars, and why you want to make it, you'll feel instantly like a millionaire even if there's only $1,000 in your bank account.

Actor and comedian Jim Carrey once dreamed of success when he was young and his father lost his job and the whole family lived in a camper van on a relative's lawn. They all took jobs working as janitors and security guards. Carrey worked an eight-hour shift after school. His attempt to be a comedian bombed and caused him to question whether he could make it as an entertainer. In 1985, broke and depressed, he drove his old Toyota to the top of the Hollywood hills. To make himself feel better, he wrote himself a check for $10 million for "acting services rendered," and post-dated it 10 years. He kept this check in his wallet. The rest is history.

Happiness and fulfillment come from reaching a point wherein you always know how to reset your mind and overcome downtimes by using positive habits you've mastered over the years. Perhaps you've learned that these downtimes are part of our lives and that we grow by bouncing back from them. If you always know that you have limitless interesting things to accomplish throughout your weeks and months, and all these things give you joy and happiness, then you know how to enrich your life. Success is perfection; happiness is embracing the imperfections.

A moment of happiness can be fleeting, yet experiencing a vast range of emotions adds to our character and helps shape our values. Fulfillment is the result of a journey defined by a deeper sense of satisfaction about the purpose of certain goals or achievements. Fulfilment matters more than happiness. Happiness is just an event, but fulfillment is deeper and most long lasting.

I recently read an article by life coach Tony Robbins[10] about six needs he believes maximize happiness and fulfillment. He talks about how we tend to equate our net worth with our self-worth.

The Need for Certainty. We need certainty in our lives because it's a survival mechanism; we need to have a certain amount of certainty to function — a sense of control about our income, our relationship and our safety, among others. We can achieve this in many ways. Some people get a sense of comfort from performing daily routines; some like to surround themselves with people they believe are smarter than they are. Other people enjoy prayer and faith so they feel they're being guided.

The Need for Uncertainty. We also need uncertainty to give our lives a sense of adventure, fun and unpredictability. This makes life less boring and more exciting with new challenges and surprises. This is how we build up our ability to face problems.

The Need for Significance. We all need to feel important, unique, powerful and special in some way. You might achieve this by buying "toys" such as cars and houses, getting more university degrees, dressing uniquely. Or you might show your compassion for certain people or organizations, giving more than anyone else.

The Need for Connection and Love. Love is something we all want and need. There are many ways to achieve it. You can feel a connection with God through prayer, or view a work of art and feel a sense of inspiration, or enjoy a pet. The need for certainty and uncertainty as well as significance and connection are fundamental needs. But the following two are the real secret.

The Need to Grow. No matter how much money you have or how many people think you're great, if you don't feel like you're growing, you'll feel like you're standing still. It's essential to step out of

---

[10] Robbins, Tony. *6 Basic Needs That Make Us Tick*. Entrepreneur.com; also on LinkedIn.

your comfort zone occasionally, because being too comfortable doesn't allow you to grow. When we grow is when we feel we have something to give.

Contribute Beyond Yourself. Anthony Robbins says that the secret to living is giving. When we get good news, we want to share it; sharing enhances what we think and feel. A feeling of personal significance does not come from anything or anyone outside us, but rather from what's inside us.

Visualize your current position, what you've achieved and what you want to achieve in the future. Be optimistic about this. You need to be grateful for your experiences and what you've achieved so far.

- Take responsibility for your actions, including for the things you didn't properly prepare for.
- Stop doing things that don't add value to your life or your business
- Stop blaming others for missed opportunities.
- Start taking responsibility for finding new opportunities
- Add new actions to your daily routine to help you reach your goals
- Keep growing, learning and improving your skills and abilities.
- Continue to shape your identity and character by defining what you want and why you want what you want.

Fulfillment is achieved by making a difference in the lives of others, so find a way to contribute and add value to other people's lives. Think of what you want people to remember you for after you die. In my opinion, being an Efficientpreneur leads to great fulfillment, because it gives you time to pursue your dreams and create a positive legacy.

**Your true merit is measured by
how much you've mattered to others.**

CHAPTER 6

KNOWLEDGE IS POWER

"Surround yourself only with people who are going to lift you higher."

— *Oprah Winfrey*

Information is the new oil. If you want to do anything in your life, start learning how to do it, because this is how you're going to discover your alternatives and discover how passionate you feel about them.

Money—and how people have earned income—has evolved over four different economic ages of humanity.

1. **The Hunter-Gatherer Age:** In the Hunter-Gatherer Age, humans relied on nature to provide wealth. They were nomadic and moved to where the hunting was good and the vegetation abundant. If you didn't know how to hunt and gather, you died. Living within a tribe was social security. Socially and economically, all tribe members lived on the same level; they all were poor.

2. **The Agrarian Age:** The Agrarian Age brought about the rise of classes. The technology to plant and cultivate the land developed, and those who owned the land became the equivalent to heads of state. Those who worked the land became peasants. Socioeconomically there were two groups, the rich and the poor.

3. **The Industrial Age:** Most people consider the beginning of the Industrial Age in the 1800s with the rise of factories, but it may have really begun in 1492 with Columbus. When he struck out to find the New World, he was searching for oil, copper, tin, and rubber. The value of real estate shifted from growing crops to providing such resources. The land became even more valuable, and three classes emerged: the rich, the middle class, and the poor.

4. **The Information Age:** Today, we live in the Information Age, where information controlled by technology and silicon produce wealth. The price of getting wealthy has gone down. For the first time in history, wealth is available to almost everyone. There are now four groups of people: the poor, the middle-class, the rich, and the super rich.

Information is valuable, but not as valuable as knowledge. Knowledge gives you the ability to filter out unimportant information and the power to act on what's essential. Knowledge, not information, is what makes you rich. Oil is valuable, but owning it doesn't make you rich. Understanding how it can make you rich is what brings wealth.

Today, you need to learn to understand how to:

- Enhance yourself esteem.
- Make yourself happy.
- Provide the best future for your family.
- Research the best way to solve a specific problem.
- Manage your company more efficiently.
- Save certain species from disappearing.
- Add value to your neighborhood and community.
- Help your country.
- Change the world.

There are many different reasons why we learn, and most of them revolve around personal or social gain, pleasure, passion, adding value, self-esteem, solving a problem or making money.

How to Learn

- Go to school to learn how to read, write and solve basic math formulas.
- Attend a professional college or university to acquire specific skills to excel in your professional career.
- Acquire and use a variety of resources about the real financial world. Learn from your own business, and any number of resources and institutions that will help you understand how to deal with money and break its code.
- Practice being more spiritual or religious to provide more balance and meaning to your life.

You can start learning things that are related to your passion. Many of us are born with artistic leanings. If you are a talented musician, you still need to study music so you can read notes or understand the history of music. The more you know, the more you can excel and add value.

The Beatles never knew how to read or write music, but they worked to enhance their knowledge continually. When you add experience to your talent, doors begin to open.

In 1960, when The Beatles were still an unknown high school rock band, they went to Hamburg, Germany, to play in local clubs. They were underpaid and the acoustics were bad. The audience didn't appreciate them, but what the Beatles gained out of this experience were hours and hours of non-stop playing time that shaped them into professional writers and performers.

By 1962, they were playing eight hours per night, seven nights per week. By 1964, the year they burst onto the international scene, the Beatles had played more than 1,200 concerts together. By way of comparison, most bands today don't play 1,200 times in their entire careers. Experience adds a lot to your learning curve and allows you to test your weaknesses as well as your strengths. If you add academic studies and professional mentorship, you become even stronger and bound for greater outcomes.

When you read books, attend seminars and courses, learn about business, success, sports, being the best speaker, managing time, you learn about life. All of these improve your life. The world is moving fast, and we need to stay current with what's going on. It's helpful to understand other cultures, be more flexible, more open-minded, and understand why people are the way they are; how their education, background and habits have shaped their current culture.

The personal development path has transformed my life. Now I'm just eager to learn more and more, because day after day I feel its power. We continue to learn what we want to improve.

Decide on the most efficient techniques that suit and support your learning, whether books, seminars, audio books, e-books, mentors, websites, university, school, experience, blogs, or online or offline courses.

Combine passive learning with active learning, which is learning by taking action.

How Books Impact Your Life

"I'm not young enough to know everything."
— Oscar Wilde

Until my late twenties, I was a terrible reader and didn't do well earning my degree in biology at the university I attended. The reason could be that I hated the educational system we had and/or that I never related to biology. I didn't like to hold a book in my hand to read. I criticized people I saw on the beach who were reading books while tanning themselves. I thought, what are they doing with their lives? Why are they wasting their time? My father told me that he never saw me as a kid read even a story about Mickey Mouse.

I learned best through experience, whether playing sports or doing something in real life. Some people in Iraq, at the time, worked in the private sector —in retail or construction — and they earned more than the doctors or engineers who were employed by the government sector. I think that people saw no point in the system of education in the country, and maybe that's what I was feeling. Most of the graduated professionals with degrees were working as taxi drivers or some other job that had nothing to do with their degrees. There was no corporate world to employ them and pay them what they should've been paid. The country was suffering economically because of the wars and government regime.

Most people were studying either to escape mandatory army service or to make their service shorter since people with a degree served less time. Even during the final years of the Saddam Hussein regime, a law stated that you could pay a certain sum of money to not serve in the army. That law was motivation for people to study. Other people studied because it reflected coming from a good family and offered a level of prestige. Families encouraged their children to study well and get good grades so they could get a degree.

I got my Bachelor's degree in biology in six years; it should've taken me only four. I graduated at the end of 2005, then moved to Dubai and did well as an employee. I made the decision that most employees make and got my MBA online with the University of Phoenix between 2008 and 2010. I enjoyed how the American system works and enjoyed studying business, finishing with a B+ average. When I completed my, I immediately quit my job and decided it was time to try my hand at being an entrepreneur.

That was the turning point of my life, when everything changed — my mindset, character, vision, the way I think and act. I started to understand that this is the path to take if you want to learn. Once you find this path in your life, you become unstoppable because once you break the self-learning code, everything is achievable.

All the books I read are non-fiction. Many people prefer fiction, because it helps them relax or sleep. Me, I'm hungry for learning and achieving, so I read non-fiction.

I think it's more efficient to absorb non-fiction information in the form of audio books or videos. When I started reading books, each one was taking me six to twelve months to finish, while audio books allowed me to finish an average of two books per week. In two hours, I can get through an information audio or video, and, for me, this is a ton more fun than reading the information in a book. I know that a book might have more details, but reading a book makes my eyes tired and, again for me, it's a slow and painful process.

Sometimes I read on an airplane trip, because there are no distractions and noise, and sometimes at the beach, but that's it.

However, you absorb material, reading (or engaging with audios and videos) is transformational, and needs to be part of your ongoing development of knowledge and education.

When I used to read actual books, I kept five copies around me – one next to the bed where I slept, one in the car, another in my squash bag, one in my living room, and another in my office. With so many copies, I had no excuse that the book was not with me. All I can say is: Read books and enjoy the transformation of your life through the unquestionable power of knowledge.

E-books Give You Control Over Content

E-books are changing the world. They are a digital form of physical books that can be easily found on the Internet in free or paid versions. Some marketers push some for their best e-books free to the market for an exchange of email, newsletters and/or subscriptions. Some famous authors sometimes promote their books by offering a limited time offer to download their book free in e-book format. Their hope is that people who read the book will promote it to their friends.

The most famous online site for e-books is Amazon.com, but there are many others: ClickBank.com, www.e-junkie.com, www.smashwords.com *and www.kobobooks.com. The development of devices or tablets like kindles is enhancing the book experience. Amazon: kindle.amazon.com or there's the Apple iBook: www.apple.com/ibooks promoting the iPad or iPhone devices from Apple, or Nook from Barnes & Noble: nook.barnesandnoble.com.*

The advantages of e-books are 1) having more control over the content of the book you're reading by searching the text of the book; 2) changing the font size to one that's comfortable for you; 3) changing the brightness of the screen; 4) adding notes or highlighting the text on any page that you want; 5) using different devices to read the same book; 6) carrying thousands of books on one device instead of one bulky, heavy book; 7) reading any of your devices without electricity since most current devices have a battery life of five to ten hours, and technology is improving on this all the time.

Although many people are shifting to digital books these days, perhaps to also save paper, you may prefer traditional, physical books. Each format has its advantages and disadvantages. Choose the one that best suits you.

Audio Books Are the Most Efficient Way to Learn Passively

Learning actively, by doing, is the most efficient way to learn effectively, but what makes it more productive is mixing it with passive learning — by reading or listening. It's been said that, after two weeks, we remember 20% of what we hear and only 10% of what we read. Also, reading consumes more energy than listening.

Audio books have been a transformational point in my learning. They've made me more efficient in my learning. I used to buy audio books at the library, but they are expensive, and a library generally maintains a limited number of titles.

Then I discovered Audible, a company owned by Amazon. It's an audio book library with great software that allows you to have your own digital library of audiobooks. They also have an app you can use on your smartphone. The way it works is you visit their site, buy the book that you want, and sign up for a subscription, if you like. Their subscription packages range from monthly to annual, and each plan gives you a certain number of credits per month. You can exchange each credit for a book, regardless of the price of that book. If your monthly payment is ongoing, you get credits you can redeem for the books you like. Or you can just buy audio books directly without buying credits, which may cost more, depending on the plan you choose.

Because these monthly subscriptions don't keep up with the number of books I listen to, I keep upgrading my subscription. I started buying an annual package of 24 credits, which costs around $229, which is nothing compared to audio or hardcover or paperback books. It's not about the cost, but also about how we can learn more efficiently.

Sometimes listening to an entire book is better than attending a seminar for a famous author. A seminar might cost you $500 to $1,000, and the author/expert usually mentions less than 10% to 20% of the content of his or her book. The book will cost you from $10 to $15, based on your plan; some books sell for less than $5. And here's a tip for you: Even if you have a plan that gives you a certain number of credits, redeem those credits only with audiobooks that cost you more than $10, because you can find some books, interviews or presentations that cost $5 or less. These you can buy directly by using your credit card instead of wasting your credits.

Of course, seminars can be inspiring and are good for networking. You can meet your favorite authors and learn new information in person. It's another way of learning, plus it's always fun to take pictures with the authors to post your credibility as an expert!

The audio book technique of learning is the best I've ever discovered. I listen in the car by linking the audible app via Bluetooth with my car audio system. If your car doesn't have Bluetooth capability, you can simply burn a CD on your computer and then listen in your car. Most of the books run an average of four to five hours; most people drive an average of two to three hours a day, so within a maximum of two to three days, you've read a book. You may prefer to listen to music when you're driving; it's often refreshing and revitalizing to listen to your favorite songs.

Some e-books are abridged; I usually go for unabridged versions. You can skip parts or chapters that you feel do not add value for you, or parts that go into information you've learned before. You'll find information repeated by many authors, but each author tends to tackle the area of expertise from his or her point of view. It can be helpful to hear different opinions about the same subject matter.

The World Is Flat,[11] the longest audio book I ever listened to (22 CDs, a total of 27 hours and 21 minutes) was irresistible, including an amazing explanation of such global forces as the collapse of the Berlin Wall, uploading, outsourcing, offshoring, insourcing, supply-chaining, and more. It's long, but I enjoyed it.

Audible allows you to return the book in case you didn't like it. Plus, they have a service you can start on your iPhone from where you stopped listening on your computer. Their app is excellent, because you can access your library through it and listen to any book you want.

Find A Mentor

At certain points in our life we feel that we know it all, but the reality is that we don't know much at all. There are times when we think we can handle a situation or process without help. This is possible, but going solo will cost you time and force you to engage in struggles on your own. If you want your journey to run more simply and easily, get a mentor.

---

[11] Friedman, Thomas L. *The World Is Flat: A Brief History of the Twenty-First Century.* NY: Farrar, Straus and Giroux, 2005.

A mentor is someone who's been through the experience you want. Having a mentor is one of the most powerful ways of learning, especially if you want to learn quickly. A mentor will guide you through a process and help you avoid most of the mistakes that he or she had to endure. A mentor will guarantee your success in a shorter period of time, with less effort and cost.

How do you find one? A mentor might be a consultant for your company, or coach for the sport that you want to excel in. You might find one for business, health and fitness issues — for anything you want to achieve.

Not every mentor can help you achieve 100% of what you want. If, for example, you hope to break a world record, having a mentor who's done it is helpful. You may need more than one mentor to reach your goal. Each one may focus on certain area of success — physically, psychologically, technically.

Listen to all views and ideas. Package them in a way that's best for you — create a recipe that represents who you are.

Just as it takes time to figure out how to select a business or new opportunity, you'll learn how to choose the best mentor. It's like selecting anything in your life; you learn with practice. Some mentors you work with might try to take advantage of you. Maybe they'll give you advice, but perhaps advice that isn't worth the value of your money. But still, you will learn.

Personally, I've experienced some bad mentors. I've seen them fade and lose their credibility and clients over time, because they were focused on making money instead of adding real value to their clients and sustaining the relationship.

In the current world of Internet marketers, many people who sell products online or offer educational courses are not experienced enough to give you what you want and need to learn. Such course instructors often provide general ideas and hammer you with technical details you might not understand, just to show you that they're "experts" in their field.

Finding the right mentor is all about research. Conducting research is one of the most important skills to develop as it allows you to find and develop whatever you want to learn.

With the Internet, finding a mentor has become an easier task than ever before. You can simply Google an expert in whatever area you wish, check that person's credibility from websites, social media pages, testimonials, review sites, or even go to the library or use Amazon.com to buy the best-selling books in any area in which you want to find a mentor.

Read books and contact the author; ask him or her to be a mentor for you. Go to www.clarity.fm — a site that features experts in a variety of areas. You can book a call with any expert you like; you'll be charged a per-minute rate for the call — charge between $1 and $10 per minute. You can ask if he or she has a long-term coaching session. Most do, so you can develop a longer learning relationship with this mentor for a couple of months, or more.

Network at Seminars

"First, you have to be visible in the community. You have to get out there and connect with people. It's not called net-sitting or net-eating. It's called networking. You have to work at it."
— Dr. Ivan Misner
Founder of Business Network International (BNI)

Seminars often spark a flame for an idea inside you after a burst of inspiration emerges from listening to a great speech or meeting an interesting person at a seminar. There are different kinds of seminars, and you can find those most helpful to you.

Some seminars last 8 to 10 hours and include a long, detailed speech often combined with a workshop or activities. A well-known author or expert — sometimes more than one — is invited to be there for the entire day. Most seminars provide time for networking between sessions. Some speaking events last only two to three hours; others are designed to pitch a product or service by an expert or author, implemented by Internet marketers.

The site meetup.com invites you to meet people subscribed to a certain interest group for a few hours. City and state governments, and other organizations provide events or exhibitions for speakers specialized in certain subject areas, and some seminars provide classes or workshops that deliver certain value.

The seminar cost varies from free seminars like those produced by TED or TEDx Talks to those that cost several hundred dollars. You can pay from $200 to $5,000, but most average around $500 to $1,000. Most often, the expert is selling something at the end of the day, or at the end of three days of a workshop. Seminars with bestselling authors or high-profile experts are priced based on a range of ticket prices.

There are seminars that inspire you to take actions that may not be the best – for example, encouraging you to spam your friends, sell them products online or share what you learn without verifying a product properly. Be careful to protect your personal credibility, as it's one of the most important aspects of your career. Share with people only what makes you confident.

The good thing about seminars is that you meet people in person and possibly develop a new relationship. I attend seminars to build credibility and take photos to post on my social media pages or websites. I like to plan certain questions I have in mind for the expert of the day. My web TV show "Be Efficient TV" has allowed me to ask any question of any expert I am scheduled to interview.

There is no such thing as a wrong question, but you need to think about what you want to ask, and make sure that it's an intelligent question. This will encourage the seminar to be more responsive to your questions.

Many experts or authors receive as much as $100,000 for an eight-hour seminar. Feel free to prepare your questions wisely; the few seconds you spend with such an author or expert might change your life forever by developing a relationship that enables access and/or opens doors and opportunities.

Even if you're familiar with the materials and subject matter, you might decide to go, if only to network with like-minded people or investors, with whom you become more familiar and who become more familiar with you.

A seminar you attend could wind up helping you market your business or idea, or get you an investor. Most seminars are advertised long before the day of the event. This gives you time to research speakers, and measure the value of your attendance.

It's possible to invite a speaker, through social media, to lunch or dinner, before their seminar. If they see, via your profile on social media or website, that you're credible, they might accept your invitation.

Developing a personal relationship takes time, and you never know what value it will produce. You might gain value after a month, after a year, perhaps after 10 years, maybe not at all. It's a long-term process. Ivan Misner, the father of networking and founder of BNI, refers to networking as a farming process rather than a hunting process. It takes time.

Share events you attend with friends — maybe even offer to buy a seminar for a friend. Attending seminars is one of the great methods for networking. Seeing people in person creates learning in a new dimension.

Learn Electronically: Webinars, Teleseminars and Podcasts

The Internet has changed the way we communicate and learn, via blogs, and online universities and courses. The speed of communication has made the world a small village by knocking down walls. These days, you can learn from home, sitting on your sofa.

You can study at many universities online, especially subjects related to business. I finished my MBA online. If you want to be a doctor, you need to practice offline in a hospital, but you can read most of your materials online. Many apps have changed the medical industry and allowed doctors to be more efficient and effective in their work.

Your kids can study at many online schools. This is extremely helpful if you or your spouse needs to travel for work, and you want your kids close to you without leaving them at home. Some argue that this can have a negative impact on your children's social life if they're not mixing with others their age; but a balance can be achieved through other social activities —sports, clubs, participating in other social activities.

Online courses have changed learning completely, since you can now find a course about almost anything you want to learn. Check udamy.com to find many courses, or Google what you want to learn and you'll find an expert somewhere in the world teaching the subject matter you're exploring. There's an online course for everything, whether you want to write a book, learn Internet marketing, how to network, or how to sell or market. Some courses take a month to complete; others, three to nine months, depending on the complexity of the course and how much time you're willing to invest.

Learning through online courses has a value that's different from reading books or blog posts. You'll see how to apply what you want to do as most online courses have tutorial videos. You see all details onscreen. Visual learning adds value to text learning. You might want to watch a video of a course while enjoying coffee or a salad. You might want to watch the TV show "Shark Tank" on YouTube, which is a great show about startups and investment. It's highly recommended to learn all the tricks you can for startups in the business world.

Another way of online learning is via webinars, which are online presentations presented by one or more experts to communicate with their customers or students. Some deliver a presentation to a certain number of invited people to a free webinar, then try to sell them a product or service by the end of the webinar. Others offer a joint-venture deal to other experts by inviting them to deliver a presentation that specifically relates to one of their own. For more information about webinars, I have interviewed webinar expert Steven Essa on my show "Be Efficient TV." You can find the show online at www.BeEfficient.TV.

Another way to learn online is via teleseminars, which are basically conference calls — like webinars, but without visuals. Sometimes you get to talk with an expert and ask questions when allowed, and sometimes it's like an interview with another guest over the phone, or a live Q&A session over the phone. With teleseminars, you don't need a computer; you call the operator who hooks you up with the live call, or you call a specific number, enter a specific code, and you get into the call.

Podcasts are another way to learn virtually. They are audio or video lectures or interviews distributed via specific online channels or platforms such as iTunes or Stitcher. You listen to them via your iPhone, iPad, Blackberry or other device. It's like radio but more targeted, as you are the one in control to choose what you want to listen to instead of just listening to something general on the radio. In the last couple of years, podcasts have been booming. Most of them are free and give you an amazing amount of control about what you want to listen to.

Offline Courses Have Their Merits

Offline courses are another way of learning. Most of us are familiar with these because they are the traditional way of learning — schools, universities, training institutes, courses and workshops. The advantages of offline learning are interaction with a teacher or professor, networking with others, and tangible relationships. Many people prefer to interact with others and learn offline, because they can question colleagues and discuss the course, directly question the professor or engage in offline circles with other students and perhaps study together.

I got my MBA through the University of Phoenix online. We could communicate with other students, but the communication was only online, since most students live in different parts of the city – or the world. Offline courses provide physical interaction with others to make new friends, create new partnerships and/or solve struggles or business challenges.

Offline courses require a huge amount of time and money. Time is wasted by needing to travel to and from the course or university and requires spending money on transportation, food and clothing. But we can't learn everything online. For example, if you want to learn how to dance the salsa or tango, you can't take an online course because such skills require practice and real-time interaction. The same is true of learning certain sports or studying medicine.

Your Personal Development Highway

Before I discovered my own personal development path, I was always scared, worried, thinking about the future and what I was going to do next in a very different way than I do now. That doesn't mean I'm not scared or worried anymore. It's just that now I know what I want to do in this life in a way that's much clearer than before. I know better how to handle challenges I might face, and that failure is more my friend than my enemy. I know that my life journey is not going to happen by default, that instead of waiting for my life to happen to me, I need to hold the reins and set this journey for myself.

The primary key to unlocking secrets is knowledge, which anyone can achieve with research. If you can do this without someone pushing you, you are unstoppable because now you are moving forward on your personal development highway.

Discovering the power of self-development has turned me into a positive person, willing to accept failure and learn from it. Even during times that I feel unhappy, I decide to read something that will teach me how to be happier. It's a simple path that can move you in a new direction.

Success comes from a mix of research, learning, personal motivation and drive to achieve certain goals in life.

- Believe that you have the ability to achieve anything
- Make a list what you need to do
- Motivate yourself to do it
- Take action
- Measure the results

Once you learn this process, you start feeling unstoppable to achieve any goal, inspire others, and create a legacy. You start to become more aware of opportunities. All you need to do is pick one that works for you — and take action.

Once you figure out your path, more ideas will pour in. More ideas are good, but you must prioritize and focus on the ones that matter more to your and to the people you want to serve. This process is all about what you're going to do to change your life. Do what works best for you — what's most efficient to deliver the best results.

You know you're on the path to personal development when you start feeling that your library is a treasure, that mentors are invaluable, that when you add value to other people's lives, your life gets ten times better — and that miracles can happen.

The more you practice, the shorter the process becomes. You'll find that your skills and knowledge will marry your ideas and that magic will start to happen more quickly. It's like when you build an Excel sheet formula — it's hard to structure it at the start, but in time, you create more complex formulas much faster by building on your main structure, without thinking a lot about the previous ones, because you've built it step by step.

The knowledge we gain by attending a college or university is basic and lays the foundation of our lives. We can add to that knowledge on a daily basis, just by reading a book, consulting a mentor, or doing research. If you look at the list of books I've read or listened to, which you can find on my blog at www.ahmedalkiremli.com/library, you'll notice that in most cases I needed to learn about a certain subject at a specific time, or that sometimes I simply read for pleasure, to expand my horizon or enhance my mindset.

To this day, the option of returning to a life of employment still runs through my thoughts, especially when struggling with certain issues in my entrepreneurial life; but the more you survive as entrepreneur, the more difficult it is to be an employee again, except in the case of a disaster.

My CV (curriculum vitae) was published on some online recruitment sites, so every few months companies find it and give me a call. At first it was difficult to say no. I always say, "Okay, send me your offer," or I ask for large compensation so they turn me down. Then I can sustain my entrepreneurial path.

I continue to believe that the employment path is riskier than the entrepreneurial path in the long run. If somebody offers you a huge amount of money, you'll still want to reject the opportunity, because you feel that even if you, as an entrepreneur, are currently making 10% of the amount offered, there is the potential of making a thousand times more in the long run. Once you take the risk, one step at a time, you'll feel the power in taking this journey and be able to realize its value.

Every human being has a different path of learning, different ideas, ways of thinking, and backgrounds. Jim Rohn, in one of his lectures, said that we don't know why only 3% to 5% of people who attend his seminars make it. We just don't know. The reality is that people can be provided with all the tools they need and still not take action.

Personal development includes tools, methods, programs, assessment, measurement systems for results, techniques, all organized to enhance your life, regardless of its financial requirements. Personal development feeds many aspects of your life — spiritual, health, financial, social, as well as such self-esteem issues such as who you are, your identity, self-awareness and what you want to do in this life.

Education Is Limitless and Knowledge Is Power

"To know is to know that know nothing.
That is the meaning of true knowledge."
—Socrates

All types of learning are valid. We all learn in different ways, but in the Information Age, we need to learn efficiently, with direction. Finding the most efficient path of learning for you can take time.

Attending a University or College

Attending a college or university is going to help shape your personality as you mix with other people. Also, there are some professions that require practice in real-life situations. Studying to become a doctor is the best example. To become a medical practitioner, you need to mix theoretical learning with practice on real patients. Learning efficiently comes from the experience of real practice.

If the goal of your education is to earn a lot of money and you check the list of the richest people in the world, I don't think you'll find a doctor on the list of the top 100 richest people, but you will find that the richest doctors tend to be those who quit their professions as doctors and build hospitals or clinics.

> *"Knowledge is power. Information is liberating. Education is the premise of progress, in every society, in every family."*
> — Kofi Annan

What made them rich is the entrepreneurial path they chose by leveraging their technical knowledge in the medical field into an entrepreneurial venture. If your passion is to become a doctor and you don't care about financial or personal freedom — doctors' working hours are difficult — that's a different story.

When working on your university degree, you may want to test your major by completing a year and then decide whether you want to continue or change your field of study. It's not wrong to lose a semester, or even a year or two. It's far better than wasting four or five years in a major you don't like, and then wasting ten to twenty more living with an unhappy career. I see many people make this discovery. Their delay is almost always caused by pressure from family or friends, more than not knowing that they've chosen a path they no longer feel is right.

Life is all about control. The more alternatives you have, the more control you have and the greater the chance that you'll have a happier life.

If you want to be an engineer, study the advantages and disadvantages of this profession. Ask yourself why you've made your choice, what you'll expect, what steps you'll take, and how this decision will impact your life. What are your alternatives in case something goes wrong?

Many mega-successfully people have dropped out of school or never got a university degree. Al Pacino dropped out of school at age 17 and took side jobs to support his desire to become an actor.

Billionaire and entrepreneur Richard Branson dropped out of school at age 16 and never got his high school diploma. United States President Abraham Lincoln left school at age 12 to work on his family farm. Actor Robert De Niro dropped out at age 16; Nobel Prize-winning physicist and *Time* magazine Man of the Century Albert Einstein dropped out of high school at age 15; Mark Zuckerberg left Harvard to complete his Facebook journey; Steve Jobs dropped out of Reed College and started Apple; Walt Disney dropped out of high school at age 16.

Other dropouts include actor Nicolas Cage, Oprah Winfrey who dropped out of Tennessee State University; Bill Gates dropped out of Harvard to pursue Microsoft; founder of Standard Oil Company John D. Rockefeller is a dropout. Jim Carrey dropped out of high school at age 16. Actor Tom Cruise is a dropout. So was Thomas Edison, the famous inventor, with more than 1,000 patents to his name for, among others, the electric light bulb, phonograph, and motion picture camera.

Actor Brad Pitt dropped out of the University of Missouri two weeks before graduation, and moved to Los Angeles where he took acting lessons and worked at odd jobs. Politician, inventor and author Benjamin Franklin was a dropout, as was Colonel Harland Sanders, the founder of Kentucky Fried Chicken (KFC). There are many more: U.S. President George Washington, Prime Minister of England Winston Churchill, actor Robert Downey Jr., author Mark Twain, Ford Motor Company founder Henry Ford, and actor Johnny Depp. They all took the risk, and won.

Books, Mentors and Experience

Doing is the most efficient way of learning. That's why we see many successful people who've never been to school but who've been successful due to their taking action, taking risks, and learning, step by step, from their successes and failures.

University learning and experience are a winning combination. You learn theoretical aspects through study and practical aspects when you act. Such advanced learning might be replaced by reading and working with mentors and might also save you some money; however, if you're planning to be an employee, having a Bachelor's or Master's degree in business is a plus. Being able to show employers a degree provides certification of the work you've done. Many employers these days care less about a university degree, especially for programmers, social media managers, sales people and other jobs that call for technical knowledge.

I think, to this day, that my degrees didn't have anything to do with my success as an employee, even in terms of getting a job, as I was never employed after I got my MBA, and before that I mainly worked in sales. My Bachelor's degree in biology had nothing to do with sales or business development.

There's never been a better time than now to find a mentor or learn digitally through courses or books due to the power of the Internet. It's easy for us to research what we want to find, and to communicate and share ideas at the speed of light. Choose tools and methods that are most efficient for you.

There are no limits for learning and education. Never stop learning until the day you die. When you talk with people, all of them agree but not everyone does anything about it. Most take no action about continuing their learning; they spend most of their day watching television or checking their Facebook wall without investing even an hour a day on developing skills and knowledge. This is why they're stuck in their lives and instead choose to observe the lives of successful people.

Invest one hour of your day learning. Listen more and speak less. Look at your problems and take action to solve them. I have friends who watch hours of football on television, then talk about it for another couple of hours on Facebook. At the end of the day, they haven't added any real value to their lives, and this addictive routine is repeated.

We all need a break through our day to enjoy life, but we need to not let the enjoyment take over the entire day, especially when we have issues and problems to solve. Some people criticize me for watching an average of four to five movies per week. I think movies add knowledge and have the power to change your mood by taking you to different places.

For me, watching football has the same action, repeatedly with no change in the scenario other than the names of the players and the type of plays. I enjoy playing football more than watching it, but millions of people get excited about it because they're addicted and use it to escape their problems in real life.

Knowledge opens the door to achieve anything you want. It is powerful and limitless, so why not spend some time every day developing yours?

I constantly struggle with focus, but I've learned to set daily goals that make me feel good. I always practice becoming better and more efficient at delivering them. For example, I have posted two to three blog posts per week or have written 1,000 words a day for my book, and recorded an interview for "Be Efficient TV" three to four times a week.

I like to accomplish the most difficult parts of my goals first thing, when I wake up. For me, the most difficult goal is writing. Once I do it in the morning, I feel comfortable and happy for the rest of the day.

The more you learn, the more you feel guilty when you're not learning. Learning becomes a fulfilling habit when you're on the right track. You cannot imagine the doors and opportunities that open for you when you engage in ongoing education.

CHAPTER 7

~

DEVELOPING YOUR FINANCIAL LITERACY

"Wealth is the product of man's capacity to think."
— Ayn Rand

Financial literacy is the alphabet of money. It's the ability to pick the best investments, make money and grow more due to your investing skills and understanding of how money works in this world.

Most of the problems in the world are financial. They're the main reason for failing marriages. Most couples do not shy away from talking about their sexual problems, but when it comes to money, they don't always discuss the issues. Some studies have shown that, in the United States, the number one fear is not terrorism but rather the fear of running out of money.

We all have to learn interest rates, types of investment and how banks operate. Money will not buy you happiness but will make things much easier. Financial literacy is a must if you want to improve your life and the life of your children in terms of stability, control and education.

Starting Where You Are

A good way to begin is to evaluate your current situation and future goals. The best way to do this is with the help of a mentor, someone more experienced than you in dealing with money. It's also wise to get advice from more than one mentor and then choose the advice your gut tells you is the most suitable for you — and take action on it. But don't stop testing.

Look at the following questions. Answering them will help you and your mentor evaluate and improve your current situation.

- What's your background?
- Are you an employee or entrepreneur?
- What's your current financial situation?
- How good is your financial knowledge?
- What's your financial history?
- Do you know how to read financial statements?
- Do you know how credit cards work?
- Do you know how taxes work?
- Do you know how to raise capital?
- Do you know how to sell?
- What's the difference between capital gains and cash flow?
- Do you know how stocks work?
- Do you know how to manage or invest in a business?
- Are you a technical person, manager or entrepreneur?
- Are you good at real estate investments?
- Are you good at investing in commodities, such as gold and silver?
- Are you good at managing your emotions?
- Are you willing to change your current situation?
- Are you persistent enough to win financial freedom, even after losing some battles?
- Are you willing to pay the price of freedom and success?

Review all these questions with your mentor. If you're seeking a mentor, contact me and send me answers to these questions through my blog www.ahmedalkiremli.com. My team and I will analyze them and determine whether I might be able to either be your mentor or help you find the right one.

Transforming your financial knowledge and experience takes time and sacrifice. A mentor can help you make the process easier, less painful, in less time and with less cost and effort. Stay away from "get rich quick" experts.

While there are many steps you may not understand at the beginning, you'll start understanding in time. Your brain may not be able to digest everything at once, so give yourself time to study, test and take action to get the experience you need.

There are some basic, technical and fundamental things everyone needs to go through. They depend on where you're starting and where you're heading.

Developing Your Knowledge of Numbers

Whether you're an employee, CEO of a large corporation, or entrepreneur running your small business, learning how to read business numbers is an essential skill. Having an accountant isn't enough. If you don't know how to read your business numbers, you'll be hard-pressed to make the right decision at the right time to end with either a cash flow or a credit disaster.

On a personal level, it's important to maintain a budget for your expenses. Whether on paper or via a phone app or computer software, you need to know how much you're earning every month, how much you're spending, and how your financial statement looks in order to know if you're going to qualify for a personal loan, auto loan, mortgage or how much money you need to start your next venture.

Using an App—You might want to get into the habit of using an app to track your daily personal expenses accurately so that you input immediately any purchase you make. This is boring and time-consuming at first, but it becomes a simple habit with time. If you have a healthy financial situation and an accountant who's tracking your personal numbers, you can use a credit card or debit card for all your purchases. Then your accountant will track your purchases on a weekly or monthly basis.

Income Statement, Balance Sheet, Cash Flow Statement—Still, knowing how to read and analyze such financial statements as income statement, balance sheet and cash flow statement is a must. These are the industry standards in terms of accounting for any business. I designed a special Excel sheet I use for all my businesses. On that sheet, I combine income and cash flow so I can quickly see how each business is performing in terms of sales, expenses, and how much cash there is on hand. Each sheet is customized per business, and based on how much data I want each manager to see for each branch.

Tip: You can download a free sample of this spreadsheet for your business here: ahmedalkiremli.com/excel.

Monthly Master Performance Sheet—I also have monthly master performance sheets I use to compare months or years of performance from both daily sheets and master sheets. Any accountant can develop an income report, balance sheet and cash flow report. You just need to know how to read and interpret them. In addition to the Excel sheets, I also use Quickbooks online accounting software to generate the three industry standards reports and additional extra detail reports.

I continue to meet managers or business owners who still don't know how to deal with or analyze their numbers. They know, generally and overall, what their numbers are, but not the details of how to generate specific percentage reports to compare monthly or yearly results, and come up with better adjustments to cut costs, improve sales, or how to improve cash flow and credit or collection situations.

All these skills are connected to being able to read and analyze your numbers to be able to make the right decisions at the right time. Most of these business owners don't know why they don't have enough cash to buy more inventory, their exact profit or loss, what's wrong in their business, or what should be done — because they are blind without numbers. Also, I met many low to medium level accountants who knows how to input data like machines and generate the three standard accounting reports but they work like machines, so if you change one transaction for them, everything seems confusing because they learned to input data rather than analyze it.

The *income statement* indicates how much money the company earns in terms of sales and other sources of income, and expenses such as the cost of sales, rent, operational expenses and net profit.

The *balance statement* details the company assets, debit, loans, liabilities, dividends or distributed profit and how much the company is worth in terms of value based on your assets, profit, depreciations and other factors.

The *cash-flow report* helps manage your cash, collections, payments for certain loads or suppliers, and enables you to be up-to-date on your cash flow so you can make better decisions and be prepared for any deal or liability.

If I were looking over a company to manage or evaluate, the first thing I would request are numbers for the past two to three years. Numbers simply tell the story and never lie, if you know how to read them properly.

If you plan to invest in any business, you must know how the business is working, be able to check expenses and sales, and read the numbers carefully to make sure everything is right to decide the right value for the company. You may want to hire an auditing team and have access to bank account and statement information to see if the numbers are registered properly, without manipulation, and that cash in the bank matches cash in the reports. There's nothing more frightening than running a business, investing in a business or examining personal finances without knowing how to read and analyze those numbers.

Three Types of Income

There are three different kinds of income:

Ordinary Earned Income — known as active or linear income — is earned by exchanging your time for cash or a paycheck as salary, wages, tips, a raise or bonus, based on whether you're an employee or self-employed. This type of income is very limited in terms of leverage and is usually highly taxed.

Portfolio Income is generated from paper asset investments such as stocks, mutual funds, bonds, interest, dividends, or capital gain investments when you intend to buy and then sell a property, business or stock. The majority of retirement accounts for many people are based on future portfolio income that comes from this kind of income, which is taxed at a lower rate than ordinary earned income.

Passive Income is generated on a regular basis from business profits, a limited partnership when you invest in a business in which you are not actively involved, franchise royalties, memberships, subscriptions, interest on saving accounts; income that comes through patent royalties, stock dividends, or intellectual property products, and real estate rentals. This type of income is the lowest taxed income, which is why it's the best kind to build wealth. This money is working for you rather than you working for the money in exchange for time. It's the most efficient way to accumulate wealth if you know what you're doing. Business owners and investors prefer this type of income.

To make more money, you need to shift from ordinary income to other types. I love passive income most, even more than portfolio income, which often appears more appealing to people as they think of buying and selling quickly by flipping a real estate deal or a business to generate capital gains. I don't like to focus on capital gains, because it involves an endless process of buying, selling and constantly analyzing the marketplace.

I recommend focusing on passive income that can generate profit and cash flow continuously on an automatic basis after building a proper system that works and doesn't require lots of modifications over time, or its modifications can be tackled by the team you've developed and the team is not also difficult to replace, or by training a new team in case something goes wrong.

Sometimes you need to modify your passive income machine, whether it's a franchise that you need to customize, or a property that you need to repaint to keep generating better rent income. But in general, the level of customization involved in passive income is much lower than with portfolio income. Plus, in most cases, passive income generates capital gains when you sell your business or property after a certain period of time. But that should not be your main goal for the deal. You should first think of the passive income of any deal, then the capital gains income. For example, think of how much continuous income a business will generate now, and how much after you build this business to a certain level. Maybe in the future you'll sell it for capital income and then exchange it with another business that will generate better passive income for you and still earn capital gains from the sell. So, your ultimate short-term and long-term goal is passive income, and capital gains goals should happen in a long- term manner to avoid a lot of flipping, speculation and customization.

Another critical point is that now, in the new era of entrepreneurship, when you create a startup as an entrepreneur and then get a salary for running the company that you've started, that's fine, if you know what to expect. To the date of this writing, I have never received a salary from any company I've founded. But that should not be your ultimate goal.

Your goal should be to become an investor or Efficientpreneur, who automates your businesses to make them work without you.

If you run your company based only on shares from the company as profit, you'll perform better than when you're salaried. Once you get a salary, even from running the company that you've founded, inside you'll still think like an employee because your work will still be connected to a paycheck.

Many startup entrepreneurs often continue to delay the launch of their companies and keep raising money because they're scared of failure. When they fail to raise more money, they try to enjoy their salaries longer to secure themselves. I think it's fine for an entrepreneur to get a salary from a company, but that entrepreneur should give up the salary for a higher percentage of the profit, or even without a higher percentage, or should step down as CEO of the company at a certain time, and enjoy being an investor and founder for the company in case there's someone who can manage the company better.

Assets and Liabilities

Basically, an asset is something that's going to add money to your wallet or bank account, and a liability is something that's going to take money out of your wallet or bank account.

When purchasing a car or a house, many people think these are assets. If you buy a car and the car has some value, it's an asset. However, the value of the car goes down the day you drive it off the dealership's lot. Plus, there are expenses you'll be paying for over time, like service, car wash, insurance, parking costs and other expenses. So, your new car is also a liability because it's going to take money out of your pocket.

The same thing is true of a new house. Home buyers believe that they're going to make money, or at least that the house will keep its value, but the reality is that you're paying the mortgage, interest on the mortgage, maintenance for the house, insurance, and for some a maintenance fee, as well as property taxes. A house can lose value in a tough economy. That's why a house is a liability unless you know what you're doing as an investor when you decide to buy the house. You need to work out a formula to see if this house is going to make money for you to consider it an asset.

If the economy is enjoying a positive trend, then yes, it's an asset. It can put money in your pocket if you rent the house for more than your monthly mortgage and other bills. If your income from home rental is higher than home expenses, you are cash-flow positive. If you buy the house at a low rate and sell it later at a higher rate, your house is an asset. It's helpful to study capital gains and cash flow aspects when you buy a house; it's advisable to focus more on the cash flow gain because it can be instantaneous and is continuous.

The same goes for when you rent an office or a building for your company. Such rentals fall under the liability column, because you're working in it and paying money for it, so it's an expense. Some companies would put it under the asset column if they own the office building and therefore consider it an asset, because they own the office and charge themselves rent in the liability column to see how much they are spending.

We all buy liabilities, but the point is that we need to keep our assets higher than our liabilities to use the extra cash to invest in more assets that will generate more income for us.

So, a successful investor's life starts by investing maybe 1% to 10% of his or her income and use the rest for expenses, assuming that income is small at the start, say $1,000 a month. He or she invests $100 and spends $900, but with the time, if this investor is doing well on investments and personal income has jumped to $10,000 a month, then he or she should not spend $9,000 and invest $1,000. Clearly, this investor's lifestyle has improved, so at the point of earning $10,000 if he or she is spending $3,000 and investing $7,000, then this investor is spending 30% of income and investing 70%. When he or she gets to the point of earning $100,000 income, the investor should spend $10,000, which is 10% of income and invest $90,000, which is 90% of income. The name of the game is investing in what you know. Do you have the right skills to win more than you lose? If you know your numbers and what you're doing, the answer will be yes.

Revenue vs. Expenses and Assets vs. Liabilities

Many people are confused about professional accounting terms. Revenues and expenses are listed on the Income Sheet; assets and liabilities are listed on the Balance Sheet.

Revenue—Whatever your company or business sells. It's income from the services you provide or products you sell.

Expenses—Costs you incur to generate revenue that you make from a sale, including the cost of making a product, salaries and rent, operating and administrating are all expenses.

Revenue minus expenses equals your profit. For your company to be successful, the amount of revenue needs to exceed expenses.

Cash Flow and Capital Gains

Investing in capital gains is buying something and holding it for a while, then selling it hopefully at a higher price. It's like buying a home or condo at a certain price, betting that the price will go up based on your understanding of the market and other elements such as location, supply and demand.

The capital gains concept is one of the most famous in the investment world. The challenge is that you always have to be under the pressure of repeatedly buying and selling, and analyzing the market and other factors when you make decisions. The process of buying and selling can be a tiring game, and the result is that you'll often suffer a more restricted lifestyle and freedom than you'd prefer in your life. That's why, these days, I don't get involved in a business for the intention of capital gain, unless I'm an investor in a project of another entrepreneur who's going through that process on my behalf. I don't like the process of having so many products to trade, because the more products you have, the more headaches you'll endure. I prefer simple concepts that involve fewer products and services, which enables me to be more focused and use the power of leverage.

As I've mentioned, my father has been in the stationery business for more than 30 years. I worked with him for a couple of years and analyzed his work. What I discovered is that the business handles more than a million items, and most stationery traders trade in no fewer than 10,000 to 20,000 items. Even wholesale traders have thousands of items to think about. When I look at his industry and the lifestyle of the traders around him in the countries in which he trades — Iraq and the United Arab Emirate — what I see is that, regardless of how much money they've accumulated over the years, those traders go to work every single day, work at least 10 to 14 hours, collect their money from the market, negotiate with most of their customers themselves, and get involved in almost every purchase of any number of thousands of items, because that's the nature of their industry.

Many single-product businesses do well these days. They're easy to market because, when it comes to manufacturing, marketing, selling and shipping, you can focus on one product. You can begin by designing a one-product business, and even if the one product later grows into five products to expand your line, it's still controllable and less of a headache than hundreds or thousands of products.

You can start a simple service business, online or offline. Service businesses can be complicated or simple, depending on the nature of your concept. It can take years to get out of a problem business. The

174 | The Efficientpreneur

simpler the product or service business, the easier you can automate and achieve more freedom in your life.

You also want to attempt to be unique. Most of the competition all over the world occurs in trading, especially trading commodities. As a result, commodity businesses have a huge number of employees, lower profit margins and more headaches because operations tend to be large and complicated.

A few months before the financial crisis that we experienced in Dubai at the end of 2008, people were buying and selling properties frenetically. You would see entrepreneurs, business owners, employees, all of them rushing to real estate promotional stands at exhibitions, malls and other places to buy properties from a project catalogue. Contractors were racing to finish an average 40-floor building in 16 to 22 months or less, because they couldn't keep up with the demand. People were buying properties on paper and selling them after two or three months, with crazy profit margins.

Trading in properties was the hot trend at that time, whether people knew something about the real estate market or not. Banks were handing out mortgages like crazy. Ordinary people and investment companies were buying properties for ten times more than the real money they had in hand, because banks were lending without proper checking on the financial strength of individuals and companies.

Everybody was buying so they could follow the buying trend without any calculations or study of the market — without any awareness that the market usually goes up and down every 5 to 10 years. There's a dip every 10 years and a huge one every 50 years for most financial markets, but people easily forget the lessons of history and think that the market will continue going up forever.

In 2007, my mother, who is an architect—talented in the technical and artistic side of her profession but weak in the commercial, business and investment side in general—came home from one of the big real estate exhibitions in Dubai. When she told me where she had been, I replied, "I hope you enjoyed the designs of the new projects and didn't rush to buy real estate, which is what most people do without calculating the risks and analyzing the market."

She responded, "Oh yes, I bought two luxurious flats, one in Abu Dhabi and one in Dubai."

I was shocked, and told her so.

She asked, "What's wrong with that? The agent at the last second gave me this great location in the building because I knew the agent through a friend. Otherwise I would lose it to the people who are queuing up for the properties from this major developer."

"Of course," I said. "The agent is a salesman and hasn't a clue about investments or analyzing the market. How much does each cost?"

"Each one costs between $300,000 and $400,000," she said.

"And when," I asked, "will these projects be completed?"

"In 2009," she replied.

Of course, once The Great Recession hit in 2007-2008, most of the projects stopped because most investors I the projects had bet on capital gains and were financing these building projects at ten times the capital they actually had on hand to invest. People stopped paying their mortgages to the banks or their installments to the developers—and developers stopped paying the banks for their loans, because people weren't paying them. The banks stopped lending, and you know the rest of the story.

To buy the flats, my mother had paid almost 50% of their value; then she negotiated over the years with the developer to combine the payment of both for one flat, and they accepted this. That didn't translate into a deal on paper because the developer was buying time to complete both projects, both of which were supposed to be finished in 2009 — then 2010, then 2011, then 2012, then 2013.

At the time of this writing, the developer just completed one of the projects in Dubai. The project is still not open as they are in the handover stage to tenants. Most of them have problems with the developer. My mom is still battling with the developer in court, and still has nothing to show for her investment after all these years. The money is frozen with the developer. According to the lawyers, we're winning the case and the developer will pay the money back plus penalties. According to the lawyers, the case was to be completed in the first quarter of 2015. At the end of 2015 my mom received a small part of her money and the rest still pending. We are now in 2016 and the case has not yet been finalized. Imagine, more than nine years and my mom's case is better than those of many other people who lost their money completely.

People usually invest in capital gains when the economy is good. Once it's bad, they lose all their money.

The other way of investing is via cash flow. You buy a flat with cash and rent it to make a return from the rent as passive cash flow after paying all the expenses of the flat, from maintenance to insurance. Or you buy a flat via a mortgage from a bank and rent it, and the rent paid by your tenant covers the mortgage payment and expenses of maintaining the flat. You make some extra money from that as well as passive income. Even if you don't make extra money and you break even, you own the flat for free after a certain number of years.

Always buy a flat that's ready to be leased, and never buy a flat on paper unless you have a lot of spare cash. Buying a flat on paper is a capital gains bet, and with real estate projects many issues occur during construction. Sometimes you don't evaluate the area well because the project is still just land and you can't get a proper overview of it. Sometimes a developer changes specifications of a project, for one reason or another. When you buy a ready flat, even if it's for a slightly higher price, you can eliminate a lot of these issues.

The same concept of cash flow can be applied to a small business you want to start. You can get a loan from a bank and pay from the cash flow of the project if it proves successful. When you start a project, think about how fast your concept can get you positive cash flow. The faster the positive cash flow, the easier your life will be by covering the bank as soon as possible. You can keep repeating the process with other branches of your business after understanding your risks. After a certain number of years, you can sell your company, or part of it, for profit, or just keep enjoying your passive income from the cash flow that you are generating.

Cash flow strategy is important because you're always secure with cash coming in, regardless of what's going on with the economy. Even if the amount of cash is less after a crisis due to a drop in rent prices or demands, if the cash flow is positive, you won't have to deal with such issues as massive drops that you see in the real estate or stock markets.

The pockets of people who gamble on capital gains are always empty, because they invest in something that doesn't produce cash for them unless they sell what they've purchased. When a crisis hits, they're out of the race. They complain about the market while cash flow investors are always in a healthier mood thanks to more strategic thinking when it comes to investments, with less buying and selling to have to consider.

With cash flow, growth is slow. It takes time to build assets that are going to produce for you — for your small oils wells that are going to produce money for you. Once you get the formula, you cannot imagine how much more powerful you'll become. You'll feel confident that whatever happens, you'll survive, because you know what you're doing and have tested that what are you doing is working repeatedly.

Once you understand the formula, you'll keep repeating it, even with a small profit; but over time, you'll make your money work for you to create passive income. You'll be out of the rat race, financially free, wealthier and less stressed. I don't know how speculators in the stock markets live their lives buying and selling every second and tracking a bunch of screens all their lives. If you have an anti-depressant supplement, I guess that where you should market it.

Your Team: An Important Asset

Never build a business that depends on only one person, even if that person is you. Building the right team is one of the most important tools for leveraging your successful business. You can't do everything yourself and need to multiply yourself to assist in your expansion and actions in some cases. In other cases, you need to hire people who can help you do the things you don't know how to do or don't like to do, so you can focus on what you do best and work *on* the business instead of in the business. Remember to avoid wasting your time on a business you can't leverage unless you're running this business on a temporary basis to put food on the table until you find a business alternative.

You can grow your team, step by step, and expand it as you grow to keep up with the competition and innovate to put the competition behind. If, for example, you have one café that you manage and then decide to open a branch, you'll need another manager to handle that branch. When you open your third branch, then you'll need a third manager. Maybe you'll decide to then hire a senior or area manager to manage all the managers of the branches so you have more time to focus on the business. More people cost more money but investing in people will save you time and earn you more money if you hire wisely and manage the business properly.

When you start making money in your business and are cash- flow positive, keep focusing on improving your team and investing in it to systemize and automate the business as much as you can. You want to be able to focus on more ventures or on growing your business into different levels. Never put all the profits of your business in your pocket before allocating a percentage to strengthening the team, improving the work culture, providing new training or hiring more qualified people.

When you work with a team for a while, they start thinking like you and add more into your ideas from their creativity and different backgrounds because they understand how you want things done and develop a taste for doing things the way you do them. Once you reach that level of communication and leadership with your team, you'll build great businesses because your dream team will be in place.

Your team is the foundation of your success in any venture. Finding the right people at the right time may be the most difficult task, whether your business is online or offline. If online, it may be easier to change team members, if necessary, and they will cost less; but it still takes time and effort to find the right ones. The same goes for your offline team, especially if you're doing your own hiring for a small business and don't have a human resources person who can focus on recruiting to save you time and effort. Many business owners underestimate the importance of HR people in a company, but experience teaches you their value.

Business owners who do everything themselves stay limited. You don't always have to do or know all the technical details of every single department of your company. You need to understand how things work in general in each department and rely on your department heads, but you should hire people who can do specific tasks better than you can, so you can focus on the big picture.

Be happy if you have people smarter than you in some of the departments of your company so you can rely on them while you focus on other demands. The team you have today may not be the right team for your company in the future. As your company grows, some of your team will grow with the company and others will not. It's best to not get emotional about having to let some people go along the way. Your business is a business, not a charity; and you employ people by signing an employment agreement, not a marriage contract. Even marriage contracts in some cases are not eternal.

Risk Analysis and Management

Risk is involved in everything, in all aspects of your life. Job security is a myth. Everything involves risk, but the point is, how do we manage it? If we're talking about investing, then everything depends on the type of investment. Maybe you reduce risk with hedging or options if you're in the stock market. Perhaps you reduce risk by purchasing insurance if you're starting a business. Maybe your business plan, research and analytics will reduce the risk of your next startup or real estate venture. Learning how to protect yourself legally is part of the risk management of any business. So is learning how taxes work for each investment. So, risk management is what you need to learn.

In the UAE, the law forces you, if you're opening a limited liability company (LLC), to have at least one local partner to whom you must give 51% of the company as a shareholder. Then you need to protect yourself by signing another side contract with a local sponsor to show that he or she is a partner — just a partner on paper — in the company, establishing a contract to sponsor you and the company. Many people ignore this step and continue without it based on trust. This is a risky step because people change over time, or maybe the local sponsor will die one day and his kids turn out to be not as good as he was. You need to calculate everything as much as you can to reduce your risk. Some people advise you to trust nobody. I say trust everybody but based on a percentage of 1% to 99%.

Knowing which legal entity to select to start your business is important. If you go with a sole proprietorship, you might be personally liable for anything that happens, based on the law of your country. The

LLC entity is liable on your behalf, so if the company goes bankrupt, your other companies will not be affected. Consult a lawyer or business expert in your city about this subject before you start a company. There are many different aspects to risk management and understanding how to calculate the worst-case scenario.

Understanding Your Country's Tax Laws

Wherever you operate or open your company, online or offline, before starting your business, you need to understand the tax laws of the city or country you're operating in, so you know if the city you're operating in is the right fit for your business.

Understanding the city or country tax law is essential for your financial success. Some countries, such as the UAE, take pre-paid fees instead of taxes. The country doesn't tax companies but there are certain costs one needs to pay on an annual basis, to renew the company's business status; and the cost varies, based on your company's activity. Some countries charge income tax or a tax on sales and services.

Investors and entrepreneurs in the U.S. and most European countries usually pay less tax than employees, so that's another advantage of being an entrepreneur. This is because entrepreneurs create jobs that will reduce a city or country's unemployment rate and support the economy.

You need to learn in which income you're operating — whether you're earning passive income, on which you pay the least amount of tax, or you're a paid employee, who pays the highest tax. This varies from country to country — some as high as 50% to 70%, others about 15% to 30%.

Understanding taxes and how they work is essential information for knowing how to do business, where to invest, how to make more profit and keep more of the money you make, instead of giving it to the government. It's always wise to consult tax experts. You don't need to understand all the tax laws of the world; focus on the city or country that you're operating in.

How to Use Credit Cards

Most financial experts or authors tend to repeat their financial advice about credit cards, which is to cut them, pay in cash or use your debit card, and stay out of debt. Credit cards motivate you to spend more borrowed money. It's difficult to control your spending habits if you use only a credit card for all your payments. If you don't pay them off, you'll keep paying interest that will eat up most of your money. Credit cards are a tool that can be used in a way that puts you deeply in debt.

However, used properly, like a loan, credit cards can make you financially free. You can use them wisely to buy things you need to operate, or participate in investments that will generate more monthly profit than the monthly interest you're paying. Over time, if you keep using them wisely, the money you get from your investments will grow.

I used my credit card to launch many of my small business ventures, such as Games Corner, the mall's number 1 video gaming corner — a simple franchise concept that provides comfortable sofas with console-based PlayStations with 3D and LED screens in corridors or other unused areas of malls. Some branches were opened on a partnership basis; others, on a franchise basis. Each branch cost from $20,000 to $35,000, which is inexpensive for a company, and that cost includes establishment of the company, and beginning operating expenses. So, I opened many branches of Games Corner with my credit cards. You can check the concept at gamescorner.com in case you're interested in opening one of your own and work with me. In most cases, I was paying interest rates to the bank, but making more money in profits.

If you've already chalked up credit card debt and want to get rid it, start paying them off one by one. Pay the minimum for all the cards you have to buy time, avoid legal action or get annoying follow-up calls from the bank. Completely pay off one of your cards, perhaps the one that's easiest to cover the full amount. Scientifically you should pay the one with the highest interest rate first, but psychologically you should pay off the one you can completely cover — to have a personal gain through a mental win and good boost to continue the process with the next card. If all your credit cards have the same balance, start by covering the one with the highest interest rate.

Credit cards charge a high interest rate. Another way to pay them off can be done by taking a personal loan from the bank to cover all the cards. Then you can focus on paying only one bill — the personal loan, and with a much lower interest rate. For example, let's say that you pay from 2% to 4% for your credit card on a monthly basis. Per year, it's 24 to 48%. This is why banks make larger sums of money from credit cards than loans. If you get a car loan, the rate is about 2% to 5% per year. If you're getting a personal loan, the rate may run from 5% to 10%. A business loan might range from 7% to 20% and maybe lower than 7% if the sum of the amount and the business investment is big. Get a personal loan, if you're eligible for one, and pay off all your credit cards. You'll avoid paying an annual 24% to 48% interest rate and instead pay 5% to 10% in interest.

You can apply for a free-for-life credit card instead of one with a specific annual fee, but it's best to get the credit card with the annual fee if you get higher credit limit and know how to leverage its use by participating in another investment that will make you more money.

Cards with annual fees offer a higher credit limit, so go with one of those if you need more money for your investment. Some banks automatically increase your credit limit every 6 to 12 months based on their automated tracking system. The higher your credit card limit, the more you can invest if you know how to invest wisely. Credit cards can save you from financial problems if you know how to use them, because they buy time, even if that time costs you interest. If you know how to use that time wisely, you can pay back the interest and make a profit on top of it.

My advice is to have more than one credit card. Sometimes a credit card gets stuck and you can't use it for some reason. At other times, you may not have a high enough credit limit on one of your cards, so you can use a backup. Sometimes the bank lowers your credit card limit, based on internal procedures that have nothing to do with you.

When the right investment opportunity knocks and you need to be ready, use as much as you can from your cards, especially if you realistically believe that your investment will get you enough profit to cover it.

Nowadays most credit cards give you 1% to 2% cash back from your purchases, either in the form of money or other vouchers to be used for purchases, so you can make money from your credit cards by paying their full amount on a monthly basis. The bank will not charge you any interest, plus you can enjoy the benefits of cash back, travelling benefits by collecting air miles, or enjoying the business and VIP lounges at airports. Some credit card companies offer you the benefit of buying one meal or cinema ticket and getting another that's free.

If you have a small business and your suppliers accept your payment via credit card for the same price you pay in cash, use the credit card for all business purchases and enjoy the benefits.

If you have many credit cards, it's difficult to track the due dates, which could make you a candidate for late payments. The bank enjoys this because you're then required to pay late fees. Be organized with your cards, and register all due dates on Evernote (https://evernote.com) so you pay on time. Also, try to avoid pulling cash from your credit cards unless it's an emergency; each time you do, you are charged extra fees.

Banks love finding new credit card customers, because they trap most people into large amounts of interest. Credit cards can be a weapon used by you or against you. This is why you need to understand how they work. Invest in your financial education first. Are you eligible for credit cards? In some countries, you're eligible when you're a student, with maybe a $1,000 or less limit. The limit goes up with a successful credit history or score.

Your credit score is connected to all the banks in your country by a central bank, so it functions like a grade for how you use your credit cards and other loans. Always keep your credit score positive to be able to get more loans or credit cards when you need them. If credit score is not yet applied in your country, this means that when you have an account or credit card with a bank, and you go to another bank, they can't see what actions you took with your first bank, in terms of credit cards or loans. They evaluate your eligibility based on questions they pose and answers you give. They usually ask for an account statement or credit card statement from your first bank for the past three to six months and evaluate your eligibility based on those numbers.

Banks become more flexible in giving credit cards during a good economy and less flexible when the economy is bad, so you need to plan ahead and use the banks as much as you can when the economy is thriving. Then, when the economy goes down, you'll be equipped with credit card funding or loans that can support your investments. The best investment opportunities tend to come in a down economy, when most people don't have enough money to take advantage of them.

Applying for a credit card is a boring process in any country. In most cases, it starts with you contacting the call center or visiting a bank to apply. Sometimes, you can ask a bank to send a credit card representative to your home or work to complete the application. Those representatives usually earn a commission for signing you up, so they fight to get you the credit card. Because the sales representative has had experience with many customers, he or she knows what the credit department will approve, so it's best to make that person your friend. Getting approval for a credit card from a bank is a game with its own rules that you will master with practice. Try calling ten banks and you'll see how much fun you can have understanding their needs. Then you'll be a master at negotiating credit card approval.

Credit cards have saved me from many difficult situations when I had to stand on my own. Credit cards are a secret weapon that can save you in difficult situations, so you must learn how to use them wisely.

Bank Loans, Mortgages and Other Capital

A **mortgage** is a loan secured by real estate or personal property. It's securing real estate under the name of a bank, which gives you the loan until you pay it off. Or, it stays under your name although the bank owns authority over the property until you pay off the mortgage.

A **loan** is a type of incurred debt provided by a bank. There are two kinds: secured loans and unsecured loans.

A **secured loan** is one in which you pledge some asset (a car or a piece of property) as collateral for the loan, which then becomes a secured debt owed to the bank, or other creditor, that provides the loan. The bank gives the loan directly to the consumer, but the property stays under the bank's name until the loan is paid off.

An **unsecured loan** — the kind we get from credit cards, personal loans, bank overdrafts, credit facilities and corporate bonds — is provided and supported only by a borrower's credit-worthiness. It's obtained without the use of property as collateral. Borrowers usually must have high credit ratings to be approved for these loans.

A bank gives you money without any security cover based on many factors that the bank's credit department sets. This may depend on your personal banking history, your company history, or your credit score if the country you're in uses a credit score system. A bank will check your banking history for the past three months to three years based on the type of loan. They'll also check to see if you have bounced checks, if you've paid off previous loans with no problems. Even though a bank loses money after all this analysis, its business is banking, so it follows certain formulas of risk to keep positive the number of loans it provides. The bank's formula changes from time to time, based on such factors as its central bank regulations, the bank's internal plan, expansion plan, and the economy.

Good Debt and Bad Debt

What people get richer every year? The answer is simple: Those who know how to work with banks and investment companies.

Banks and many lending companies don't want to share the profits of your project with you; they just want to lend you money based on your previous financial track record, and collect an interest rate from you while you pay back their money over an agreed period.

Good debt occurs when you know how to use the bank's money or a lender's money investing in an asset or business that will generate more money for you than the interest rate you pay.

Bad debt happens when you use the bank's or lender's money to invest in a liability that will take money from your pocket, such as a car that breaks down, or an unsuccessful business or property that you're paying for — where your expenses add up to more than what you're making from income on the property.

The beauty of using other people's money, whether loaned from a bank or from people you know, is that you can leverage the power of that money for your idea without investing your own money. But, you do need to be credible enough to encourage people to invest in you or your project.

Raising capital from other people might involve them as partners in your company. Having investors and partners in your business can add qualities to your company that can range from expert advice to a network of connections. If things go well with your project, then it becomes easy to raise more capital from the same investors for your current project or for a new venture. When you form solid relationships with investors, you don't have to be concerned with anyone needing to re-evaluate your credibility. Banks are different. Even if you pay them back their previous loan, they will still ask to evaluate you over and over again on any new project. If you have a good history with that bank, it will be more flexible with you over time. Still, at any time, the economy or some new internal rules could change how they evaluate.

To create financial freedom and wealth, you need to learn how to use other people's money to acquire more money, use the banks, and take advantage of what they have to offer.

Choosing How to Invest

"Here's how I think of my money — as soldiers — I send them out to war every day. I want them to take prisoners and come home, so there's more of them."
—Kevin O'Leary

Bootstrapping is a term used for people who invest their own money into their business venture without getting money from an external source such as family and friends, angel investors or venture capital firms. It gives you full control of your business in terms of decisions and equity, plus there's no pressure from an external investor to do anything. It usually limits you from expanding in the amount of time you would like, due to the limitation of capital, but that's not a bad thing. In most cases it makes you more patient in growing the business, proving that your concept works, and makes the next stage of raising capital easier.

Raising capital from family and friends is where most new entrepreneurs start. If your family and friends don't believe in your business idea, it might be difficult for investors to invest in you.

However, that's not always the case as it's possible that your family and friends are not experienced enough to understand your business model, or they may have limited cash to invest in your business. A problem that often arises when using the money of family or friends is that your business relationship can affect your life relationship and create a different perspective — sometimes positive, and negative, especially if the business is failing. If the business is making money, a change in life relationship still occurs and tends to create a more formal relationship.

Angel investors and venture capital firms invest money in different ways. Angel investors invest smaller amounts than venture capitalists and usually get involved at the beginning of a project. The amount an angel starts investing can vary from $10,000 to, say, $3 million. Some will go higher. Venture capitalists always go for larger amounts, usually from $2 million to $3 million minimum, and up to $50 million or even $200 million. They tend to get involved in a business after it's a proven concept. They like to see that your business is making a profit or at least has a positive cash flow and just needs more money injected into the infrastructure to fire up the process of making more money. Some venture capital firms do invest in early stages of companies, but less often.

Venture capital companies are more proficient in terms of investing. They have a larger group of experts who can advise and help in your operations. Angel investors are individuals who want to invest with you. It's not that they're not professional or disciplined — some have managed a business, some not; some are professional self-employed people, such as dentists, doctors or engineers, who earn well and want to invest in more ventures.

Venture capital companies want more control, either by having a larger stake in the business to control its decisions, or at least by holding one seat on your board of directors. Usually venture capitalists assign somebody from their company to be at your board meetings. They get involved in the operations and may even support you with operations that put you under their radar but can be good for business, even though not all entrepreneurs appreciate this. This is why some entrepreneurs find a larger company to be less fun than a smaller one. The larger the company, the more politics and pressures will arise.

Angel investors don't want to get involved in your business in terms of management and operation. They generally are interested in investing in you and simply want a return on their investment. In most cases they aren't interested in a seat on the board or getting involved in business decisions. However, they are supportive in case you need help. Some simply like being silent partners and enjoying financial freedom without getting involved.

It's sometimes necessary to babysit angel investors and be more careful with them, because they don't have the emotional intelligence for business, especially if they are still at the early stages of their investing career. They may want to get involved by asking many questions during the process of developing your business, so you need to know how to choose partners who understand the challenges you might face. It might be good, in partnering with people, to set some systems for communication in advance, such as meeting monthly or on quarterly basis, or providing monthly or quarterly reports. It takes a while for investors of any kind to trust you and work with you without constantly bothering you. You need to remember to protect your credibility on an ongoing basis, as it's one of the most important assets you have.

When you approach investors, there's no need to be scared that your idea will be stolen, especially if they are professional investors who review hundreds of business plans per year and don't have to time to copy, nor are they interested in copying, other people's ideas. If you wish, you can ask them to sign a non-disclosure agreement, or some sort of other agreement, before sharing ideas with them. Many venture capital firms don't like to sign such agreements and sometimes won't review your business plan if you ask for an NDA, because most of them don't have time and don't want to get involved in legal formalities. But if it makes you more comfortable, especially with smaller investors, people you don't know, you can always ask.

You need to be straightforward with your investors and you need to thank them for their trust. You need to be frank about possible challenges, such as what happens to money when disasters occur. You need to show that you're in control of your business and you know what you're doing. This is how you build a relationship.

You need to be aware of the time you have to raise capital for your idea. When real time becomes a factor, you don't want a situation wherein nobody shows up. It's good to build a large network of investors, so you have alternatives in terms of financing a project within a short period of time; otherwise you could lose your opportunity and that's fine as that's how you learn and adjust to start over again more intelligently.

In conclusion, bootstrap your business idea if you can at the start. Grow it to a certain level, then go with family or friends, or with angel investors directly. You can make this happen by getting involved with an incubator or accelerator who will invest a small amount of money in your startup at early stage and own from 10% to 15% of your business but provide you with a great amount of information within a three- to six-month program. This can help you in most of the aspects of your business and even sometimes get you introduced to a community of entrepreneurs, mentors and investors. Once your business starts generating some good money, you can pitch a venture capital company. Some entrepreneurs like to keep things small by not involving investors. There are fewer headaches and less pressure when you use your own money with no investors involved, but in most cases, you stay limited in terms of size. So, choose what works best for you. Whatever road you choose, mentor and expert advice is always highly recommended.

Being Rich and Being Wealthy

Wealthy people are rich, but rich people are not necessarily wealthy. Wealthy people have sustainable wealth over a longer period of time than rich people, who can be rich for a certain period of time and then suddenly aren't rich anymore. So, measuring wealth is about how long the money will last without your having to work for it. It's about how passive income works for you – the ability to keep making money without your physically doing much to earn it, and maintaining your lifestyle and standard of living.

Wealthy people are not only rich in terms of money, but have rich minds; they impact people around them, they like to change the world and make it a better place than the place they've known; they have a vision and a sense of mission inside them to do good in the world and change people's lives. They're not selfish in terms of thinking or money; they want to teach and benefit the people around them by adding great value to the world. Wealthy people are not only motivated by money but by dreams, passion, purpose, and make a difference in the world by leaving a legacy behind them. Wealthy people like to be remembered by a great achievement that has made a difference whether it's a book, an invention, a way to save certain species, or a certain form of charity for a good cause.

Wealthy people are rich in knowledge. They like to learn and keep learning until they die. They like to pass their learning on to others. Wealthy people break the codes and secrets of wealth so they can keep making more in order to do more good and enjoy the game making money beyond the sake of accumulating more of it. Wealthy people don't work for money; they make the money work for them.

Rich people sometimes know how to make money but don't know how to keep it; they spend whatever they make. That's why you sometimes see celebrities, athletes or lottery winners lose their money within a couple of years. The wealthy are financially free people, and have acquired good financial education to get to that level. They know how to escape the rat race that traps many rich people in an endless, pointless self-defeating process.

Wealthy people are also rich in the daily habits that make them the way they are. They have discovered who they are, what they want to do with their lives, and why they want to do it. Rich people believe that money is everything in life; we often see them unhappy and unfilled, even after making a lot of money.

**If you focus on your wealth of knowledge
and learn to add value to other people's lives,
the money will follow.**

CHAPTER 8

THE TRANSITION: HOW TO FOLLOW YOUR "WHY"

"The two most important days in your life are the day you are born and the day you find out why."
— Mark Twain

Many people don't know why they want to do something, even if they have a sense that they want to do *something*. They don't know why they should take the next step in their lives. It's like people who can't decide which movie to buy when they reach the cinema counter. If you've ever stood behind one of them in line, you know what I mean.

Study your moves and plan them properly without blindly throwing yourself into unknown areas. Sometimes you want to learn from the adventure, as it comes, but it's still advisable to figure out what you want, know yourself as much as you can, know that you may be jumping into hell, and that you'll be fine since that's where you'll learn more than you possibly could in your comfort zone.

Some people make the transition without knowing why, some have plans, and others set plans but realize they're not right.

**Ask yourself why you want to make the transition;
then set your goals.**

It's fine if your goals stretch and change every few years. The more you learn, the more your goals develop. Define what you need and feel.

- What is your inner voice telling you?
- Are you fed up with your job?
- Is it the money?
- Are you unhappy?
- Is it security?
- Is it freedom?
- Do you want to change your life?
- Do you want to serve others?

If you want to earn money, you need to think about creating a product or service that adds value to others before thinking about yourself. It's good to think about serving others and helping them solve their problems as a way to generate money.

If your reason is happiness, you need to discover what you really enjoy; then keep doing more of it. If you're a successful employee based on your definition of success, you'll be happier than a messed-up entrepreneur, so keep being an employee if you don't think you want the pressure of being an entrepreneur. Happiness is not just about changing. It's about knowing what you love to do. It's being passionate about where you're heading. If you trust your inner voice and believe you're on the right path, then you are on the right path and, step by step, you'll make discoveries.

If you're looking for freedom, security will not give it to you. You have to let go of security in order to have the freedom you want.

Even if you're very rich but must be surrounded by guards just to go to a restaurant, then where's the freedom? If you never leave home and hide from everything and everyone, you'll never have freedom or happiness in your life. You'll always have the fear of insecurity and imprison yourself to secure yourself. This is not the best definition of security.

You need to think about freedom from a totally new perspective, because freedom is priceless. Some prisoners have a stronger free spirit than people who lock themselves in their workplace, so you need to change your mindset to make the transition work for you.

Some transitions trigger tough times, so you need to be reminded that you may have to sacrifice, cut your expenses, sell some of your assets and control your emotions to make progressive steps towards your goal. Building an empire takes time, effort, sacrifice and a lot of sweat in the beginning to build the right system that will raise you up and give you the freedom you seek — later. Dream big, but start small.

My final advice to you before making the transition from employee to another job, or from employee to entrepreneur, is to think long term about the effect of making this transition. I think efficientpreneurship is the right path — painful in the beginning, but beneficial in the end. Also remember that if you want to feel happier and safer, keep creating more options. Being an employee simply cannot give you room for many alternatives.

On Which Side of the Table Do You Want to Sit?

Being an employee and being an entrepreneur — each has its own advantages and disadvantages. It's time for you to evaluate which side of the table is best suited for you, based on your mindset, goals, and current or future financial plans. We're all eager to grow, but at different levels, and that's what makes us different from each other based on our background, knowledge and experience.

When you're an employee, hired for a job, if you do well in your position, you're likely to feel, after a while, that you ought to be promoted to a higher position. You might then feel the need to move higher by becoming a manager, then director, and so on up the ladder. At a certain point, you may start to feel that employment life is not exciting you anymore, because you've learned what you want to learn and your current workplace is not feeding your hunger for growth anymore. Perhaps now you feel confident enough to make a quantum leap and start your own business, plan a work discovery trip, or whatever your passion, purpose and inner voice is driving you to do.

On the other hand, maybe the employment side of the table is best because it fits what you know, based on your financial challenges, knowledge and skills. Still, most of us, on one occasion or another, want to grow, and shift to where there's a higher level of financial freedom and time, if we plan properly, to take risks and stay open to learning.

Before jumping into the entrepreneurial life, you need to take baby steps of understanding. I've already said this more than once, but I want to stress that you'll need to be prepared to face challenges you've never faced. You'll want to read about the industry you're getting into, and also about how to manage and market new ideas.

Read at least three or four books about your subject of interest by different authors, to get a variety of perspectives. Some people jump into "get rich quick" programs and end up disappointed because so-called gurus claim to know a lot but, in fact, have been in the industry for a short time.

There's no "get quick rich" formula for something you're just getting into. The speed of your success in any industry is based on your background, knowledge, skills and experience. You might be a perfect match for a certain industry, but not for another. When you're a perfect match, the speed of achieving success will increase based on your understanding of what you're doing, your added value to the market, market size, the amount of focused action that you are taking and the quality of your idea.

Some employees want to be promoted into higher positions or make the transition to entrepreneur to be the boss, to feel they're important, to meet more principal people, or manage a greater number of people. The question is, when you reach this goal, will you be fulfilled? Will you enjoy this life? By adding value to others, will your way of thinking shift into other interests that will surprise you?

The key to more success and fulfillment is to keep learning, no matter at what side of the table you wind up taking a seat.

Why Most Entrepreneurs Quit

There are several reasons entrepreneurs decide to not be entrepreneurs. One is fear — fear of losing, continuing a questionable journey, or taking responsibility for management. This happens with business people who attempt to run their business on their own, trying to be the visionary guy, the manager, the technical guy, and the bootstrapper or investor. Trying to put all of these elements in one person is difficult when you start a company. It creates a lot of pressure.

Learning to Delegate

You need to delegate — to replace yourself. That can't be implemented without a plan in advance, unless your plan is to slowly grow the company within a long period of time. To be successful is to know how to hire the best people and how to use them. You want to hire people possibly more experienced than you for certain skills, which adds value to the company. You can start a company by yourself, but not wait too long to hire and delegate some tasks until you reach the full automation model — or become at least 50% to 80% automated.

Nowadays, even online startups require a team — sometimes a larger team than an offline business.

Lack of System

Another reason that makes many entrepreneurs quit has to do with, intentionally or unintentionally, creating their new business as a trap for themselves as employees in that business. They will experience more headaches and responsibilities than they had in their job, because they've not built an automated business model that works without them. They end up working longer hours in the business instead of on the business. After a certain period, they get tired and decide to return to employment life because they didn't know how to build the system, right from the beginning, so that it can develop over time.

Finance, Capital and Accounting

Entrepreneurs must know how to differentiate between income, capital gains, cash flow, debt and expenses. They must know how to manage the collection process, how to refinance their business with a bank or other investor, including the possible need to raise more capital in their plan. They must plan a budget that will help them survive for at least a year, to test the project. They need to not expect to make money from day one after opening the business.

The "Get Rich Quick" Dream

Building a business requires a lot of planning, hard and smart work mixed with proper execution and marketing for a certain period of time, to take the business to the next level. There's no getting rich quick when starting a new business.

Starting Too Big

My ongoing advice is to think big, but start small. If you're a new entrepreneur and don't have a lot of experience, start small so you can shift, modify, correct, and learn.

Developing Emotional Control

Controlling your emotions as an entrepreneur is one of the most important skills you'll need to master. You'll face problems, dips, rejection, and other obstacles for which you need to be strong, prepared, and ready to calculate any worst-case scenario. You need to be tough to handle all the challenges you'll face, and that's impossible without having control over your emotions.

Increasing Managerial Skills

Management is about solving problems. In most entrepreneurial ventures, the business owner is the one who handles management of the business. The business manager will solve multiple problems every single day, dealing with employees, payroll, marketing, troubleshooting, resources, quality, standards, and more until the company can start affording more quality staff to reduce pressure from the manager.

Insisting on Loving the Business

Some entrepreneurs get bored with the idea of their venture and get less excited about it over time. For me, implementing an idea is not necessarily a fun thing to do. It's not a must that you love the idea you want to implement.

Some people say just do what you love — but I say that while it's a good thing to do what you love, it's more important to do what's going to work.

Many people love what they do, but don't know how to generate money out of it. The numbers are what you should care about first when you start a business, unless it's a charity business. I still have businesses I love but some don't perform as well as others I don't love. While your heart tends to live closer to the ones you love, you need to remember that your investors care about making money, and they are the ones keeping you afloat. I have learned to build businesses that work, and I don't care if I love them or not, as long as they're successful and making money.

The Importance of Financial Education

Financial education is the roadmap to success as an entrepreneur, or even an employee, because even if you're an employee you'll use your financial education in some investments. Any subject connected with money requires some sort of financial education to excel in it.

Many entrepreneurs quit their jobs too soon because they get excited about jumping into the entrepreneurial life. Then they wind up caught in the reality of new challenges. They don't know how to cover their basic expenses and have a continuous fear of repeating the journey.

Adding Value Is Vital

Some entrepreneurs think only about polishing themselves instead of about the business. When you build a business, you need it to help others — not only you — in order to make money. People care about what value you're going to provide them. Adding value in business is critical to a business's success. This is the first thing to think about when you design your venture.

Sales, Marketing, Persistence and Focus

Some entrepreneurs quit because they lack sales and marketing skills, which are critical for an entrepreneur. Everything starts with sales when you want to shape a company. This is how people get to know about your company and its products. Sales are what shape your company and lead to your growing more departments — from accounting to human resources and beyond. These departments service the pressure that sales put on your company, which is why you see most companies begin with one guy trying to sell a certain product.

As an entrepreneur, you need to keep fighting. Some would-be entrepreneurs quit in a short time without realizing that they're close to success but weren't persistent enough to pursue their dream to the finish line.

Starting a new venture leads you through many ups and downs; persistence is mandatory.

It's difficult to stay focused in today's world, as the noise in our lives increases every day. Many entrepreneurs jump from one opportunity to another without focusing on what they want to achieve and how they want to achieve it. This leads to keeping them limited in their accomplishments without diving into real success. Many focus on the competition more than on what they want to implement. Then they quit without trying.

Your Adventuresome Spirit

Risk is the main dilemma for employees. Their complaints are either that they don't have money, or that business is a risky thing. All I can say is, from my personal experience, what I've seen happen with many people, and what I've read and researched, being an employee today may be the riskiest long-term path.

Let's say you're an accountant in the oil and gas sector and accounting is a general specialty that can be practiced in many different industries. You're on your career path and improving year after year. The bad news is that if you're lucky enough to survive 20 years without getting fired, and at age 50 a crisis hits because of the economy and you get fired at that age, how do you earn a living?

The economy goes up and down all the time. You may not lose your job because of the economy. You might lose it because your manager likes someone new. Maybe the new manager doesn't like you and will fire you or force you to quit. Sometimes company owners change top management or merge with another company, which affects management, environment, salaries and staff.

You might lose your job for any number of reasons; nothing can guarantee that you're going to continue at any job long term. Maybe you're not qualified enough to continue if advanced changes have been made. Maybe the company outgrew you in terms of knowledge and expertise and you can't develop your skills.

A friend, who used to be a pilot, once said that pilots are like bus drivers. The only difference is that they drive in the air in a nicer toy filled with gadgets. The main problem is that when you're 50 or 60 years old and lose your job and all you know how to do is play with those buttons and gadgets, what's your backup plan? At this age, you learn more slowly, and you're less interested in taking new action. As we've already discussed, as an employee you're likely to have one specific skillset, something you know how to do in-depth, but once you start swimming out of your comfort zone your floating is highly questionable.

Both the employment and entrepreneur paths can be risky, but by making mistakes, learning and taking baby steps, you can overcome challenges. Employees tend to work toward avoiding making mistakes to be perfect at what they do; they stay focused in their limited area of expertise. Entrepreneurs make mistakes by experimenting with employees and push them to be better in what they do in each department, experiencing a greater variety of responsibility.

**Regardless of how much knowledge you have,
any business faces risks, but the point is to know
how to manage risk and minimize it.**

The Cost of This New Journey

"Pizza made me who I am. In the summer of 1998, I dropped out of college and started a pizza restaurant called Growlies in my hometown in rural Canada. My seed money: a credit card with a $20,000 limit."
— Ryan Holmes

If you want to take the journey of transitioning from employee to efficient entrepreneur, you need to pay the price. The big question is: What will it cost?

The price is:

- Having to learn new ways to work.
- Facing an ongoing life of change.
- Being out of your comfort zone.
- Networking with groups of people you don't know.
- Getting accustomed to entrepreneurial environments.
- Continually polishing your skills.
- Learning how to sell.
- Learning how to raise capital.
- Working more hours on your idea for free.
- Sleepless nights.
- Failing repeatedly.
- Facing people who say, "I told you so."

Some entrepreneurs pay the price of sleeping on the sofa of a friend's house for months, or living on food stamps.

Don't expect to break through and be successful at your current stage, which is called "wantrepreneur" – that's wanting to be an entrepreneur – without knowledge, without spending time learning new information, without new experiences, or stretching yourself and struggling, failing and standing up again.

The price you pay may be money. But it could also be a full year of emotional struggle, or wasted time. Are you ready to pay for this giant step? Your plans, goals, achievements and numbers will tell over the time.

How Many Times Do You Need to Go Broke?

I've been broke in my life many times, sent back to zero, and sometimes thousands of dollars less than zero. I call those the restart times. What really matters is what you've learned through that experience — how to come back and stand on your feet again.

One of the reasons I could come back was due to my learning how to invest. I continued to be broke for a couple of years because whatever I was making I was re-investing and testing with a new idea or business. Some failed and others worked, so I never had ongoing cash flow. Sometimes you need a certain level of cash flow to be able to finance other projects. But when you're in the early stages of a breakthrough, restart times might repeat more than once until you find your own magic formula of success. I like to always use hope to fuel the achievement of my goals.

Many times, I've been in a situation with a tiny amount of cash flow, and still invested up to 70% or 80% of what I was earning. That process can move you into the zero zone, but at the same time it inspires you to succeed. Without stretching yourself, you stay limited, but of course when you have a family to take care of, you need to be mindful of your stretching.

Even if you're not building businesses or systems, it's normal to fail and go broke. Being broke is not a bad thing. This is how you're going to learn, and this is when you start from zero and have nothing to lose, so your motivation level is high. Pressure shakes us up from time to time, which can be good, because that's when most people decide to take action toward what they want to achieve.

Returning to zero a couple of times is part of the learning process. Do it quickly! The younger, the better, because when you're young, you're more flexible. You're more likely to discover new limits and take more risks since you have fewer responsibilities. People in their 20s have amazing drive, and tend to be fearless. So, get on board as early as possible in your life so that for the rest of your life you'll enjoy the wisdom you gain from these experiences.

This will be a priceless experience that you'll always appreciate and never forget. But, of course, at the time of the crisis you'll hate yourself, and lose belief in yourself. But later, when you look back and connect the dots, you'll realize that this is what made you who you are — stronger, wiser and more successful.

So being broke is a normal thing. What is abnormal is continuing to be poor, because poor is something that's difficult to bounce back from. Real entrepreneurs bounce back.

I'm not rich yet, but I'm financially free. I know I'm going to be very wealthy; it's just a matter of time and more experience. I broke many areas of the money code but need to tune my process to break it completely. Before you break the money code, you must first break many other codes, such as how to learn efficiently, have a vision, be persistent and fight to achieve your dreams. One aspect to keep in mind when you break any code is time. You're learning, but how efficiently are you learning to achieve your goal within a certain period? Your primary goal is to first become financially free.

Being broke is a temporary thing. Being poor is going to continue unless you take steps to change. It's completely fine to be broke.

**The point of being an entrepreneur, a real entrepreneur,
is to know how to bounce back from any failure.**

I know now how to bounce back from disaster situations. When I think that I don't know, I figure out a way. Two things nobody will take from you are your learning and your ability to survive. I might lose money and make mistakes, but nobody will take away my experience of bouncing back. That's why I'm no longer scared of going broke.

Once you're confident that you'll have no trouble bouncing back, you'll be fearless.

Start Your Transition with a Backup Plan

"Control your own destiny, or someone else will."
— Jack Welch

When I began my career as an employee, I jumped from job to job. At the time, I didn't realize the main reason for my constant job changes — I thought the reason was to find a better position with more money. This is what most employees think when they change jobs.

After several such jumps, I went back to a company that I had worked for before, for 40% less salary than I was earning from the company I'd been working for. That's when I realized that there are many reasons to change jobs. Money is important, but it's not only about money. When you accept a job, you also need to think about comfort and happiness, you need to ask yourself is this new job going to teach me something new, is it going to add value that I can benefit from in the future? Who's my direct manager, what's the environment like, and can I work within it?

If you're thinking of changing jobs, realize that most companies operate in the same way and have their own politics and policies, some of which you may not like. If you work for a multinational company, you'll find a better environment and you'll learn more, but is your goal to continue in your current career? Is this the only path you want to consider?

Stay eager to search for another meaning, another option, or another channel. Stay hungry for new things and experiencing different possibilities. Question everything. Keep digging for answers. When you get close to the right answer, you'll recognize it once you get confirmations from experts in the field you're exploring.

Before quitting your job, think about your backup plan. Don't quit your job after getting super-excited after attending an entrepreneurial seminar, or because the speaker was talking about making millions of dollars in a year. Plan well before taking any action, set the right goals, work on your entrepreneurial idea while you're still employed by dedicating extra hours to it. If you want to escape the rat race and achieve your goals, prepare to sacrifice and test the potential of your idea before jumping in full time.

Work for free just for the sake of learning. Many people will give you a job if you offer to work free for them. Be honest and tell them that you're doing it to learn. Some people work for free to demonstrate their capabilities so they might be offered a job later with the same company. Working for free is an amazing experience. It makes an employer see you as a leader because you're strong enough to work without pay, to show your potential, for personal achievement, or to learn how to open your own business.

It's an interesting time to start a business. Many tools and mentors are available, and it's easy to get any information you want from the Internet or other sources.

This recent easy access to information has changed the game and leveled the field.

Create a business plan, consult mentors, set goals, attend seminars related to your venture, read several best-selling books about the area that you want to jump into before quitting your job, and study the market potential. Study all the obstacles and challenges that you might face before jumping into an area that might be foreign to you.

Set A Deadline to Make the Transition

Regardless of your goal, you need to set a deadline so you can take action to achieve it. If your goal is to make a transition from employee to efficient entrepreneur, you don't have to quit your job tomorrow and achieve it today. Set a deadline of from one to five years. Then start working on your idea before you quit your job. Create a step-by-step process for every single day based on the plan you've designed.

What will be your first step? A website? New app? A kiosk project, retail shop, or laundry service? Act on this idea based on your roadmap to achieve it, and keep evaluating your progress until you reach the finish line.

**Creating a deadline is essential for achieving any
goal you want to achieve. It will motivate you and
hold you accountable to achieve your goal within
the time limit you set.**

If you can't achieve your goal within the time you set, this is normal. It happens to all of us. Create an extension for your goal. Make lists, keep calendars, create mind-map programs. You may still fail, but making any progress helps you excel. I use several programs on my Mac and iPhone to help me set and act on deadlines like iCal for appointments, iMindMap to design an action plan, 2do for to do list, Evernote for notes and Asana for task management with my team, and will talk more about these in Chapter 10: Tools, Techniques and Resources.

Investing in a Business

I have avoided talking about such areas of investing as real estate, paper assets and commodities. I'm an expert in business and not in these other areas of investment. Still, many people make money in these areas. My advice is to invest in what you understand rather than what appears attractive. While business is the most rewarding area of investments, compared with the others, it's the riskiest.

The reason I like business most has to do not only with the rewards, but also the control. Control is a major factor on your path to financial freedom. In business, you're in the control seat more frequently than in the other three areas. The market goes up and down, but in general you can make decisions and changes. In stock or commodities markets, you have less control, as it's difficult to predict the market even after you study it, but people do make money in these areas if they know what they are doing.

In the paper assets and commodities markets, you need to be aware of many variables all the time, which is time-consuming. You need to track news related to the industry you're investing in, news about the world economy, supply and demand, news about terrorism and other mind-consuming information that you would rather not know. The paper asset market is a fool's game that sucks money out of people who don't know how to invest in other areas such as business or real estate. The smart people involved in the stock market are with the companies that succeed in reaching the state of initial public offering (IPO) to raise money from the masses and multiply the value of their companies by ten- or even a thousand-fold. The smart participants in the stock market are the mutual funds companies who take your money, gamble with it, and share with you only the profit while you suffer all the loss in case there is loss. Some still earn some fees even when you lose.

After business, I like real estate because it's more predictable than the paper assets or commodities markets. The primary problem with it is that a large chunk of money is required to get in, and usually the rewards are small. However, in the long run, it provides good capital gains and can also give you a good cash flow from rent if you know how to raise capital from the banks and invest wisely in a proper location. If a business works properly, it will enjoy much greater rewards than are possible with real estate. In some cases, less money is necessary to get in, especially now that we're in the Information Age, when you can start many businesses with a low investment cost.

With real estate, if, for example, you have 10 flats, each earning you $1,000 a month after all expenses, that's $10,000. With this amount, most people can retire. The problem is that people sometimes get bored. If they know real estate well and are already getting the $10,000 a month cash flow from rent, they may not want to keep repeating the process to invest in real estate. Instead, they may want to sell one of their properties, let's say for $200,000 and try to get into a business.

Most people aren't patient enough to stick with what they know and continue repeating their process to accumulate wealth. It's best to not be within this group of people. Sometimes we all need to dabble in new areas, but at the same time we need to manage our emotions — use our mind and gut more than our heart when it comes to business.

I tried once to invest in paper assets and to trade in Forex (foreign exchange market), a global decentralized market for trading currencies. In my opinion, it's an annoying life since you must check the market constantly. You'll find that you can't sleep at night because these days you can access the market from all digital gadgets such as pads and phones, so people check more than ever. I don't see that as an efficient way of living a relaxed lifestyle. Some investors trust certain companies to trade for them in the stock market, and they unplug from the market because they're doing well in other areas in which they invest. They check once or twice a year, then, based on the numbers, decide whether to continue investing or not. Those people are long-term investors, not speculators.

When you fail in business, you learn and adjust. This is why you see big investors, who build a great amount of wealth, invest some amount in real estate. It makes them money, with less risk than business, to diversify. They give some money to companies or friends they trust to invest for them in paper assets or commodities, but most of them come back to investing in businesses, because while business is riskier, it's the most rewarding and controllable. Over time, your learning curve in business grows, you gain more control over your emotions, and you get smarter about choosing the best businesses. In the stock market, regardless of how good you become, you'll never have full control because the market has the upper hand in terms of control.

Types of Businesses

By now, you've decided to choose business as your vehicle for transition from employee to efficientpreneur and to build your financial freedom. Before choosing a business, you need to know what alternatives are out there.

Home-based Business. Starting a business at home is great but doesn't work for everyone. Can you motivate yourself, especially if you're starting a business by yourself? Is your home the best place to start your business? If you have children, or other family, it might be difficult for you to focus, especially if your flat or house is small and doesn't have enough rooms to isolate you so you can properly focus on the business. Would you be able to balance your work with your family life?

Starting a business at home can give you more flexibility and time with family. Any business you start that doesn't work for you at home you can shift to another location at any time in case the business is working well and covering its expenses.

Some people find it depressing to work from home, especially if they live alone and find it difficult to self-motivate. You need to know yourself, your strengths and weaknesses. A home-based business can be an online business that services, trades, or sells physical products, such as cakes, for example.

Family Business. Starting a family business has the advantage of having one or more family members helping you, sometimes without pay. Another advantage of a family business is that you tend to have more trust in the people you're starting the business with. That's not always the case, but in general, family businesses have the advantage of being strong, and in control, because of the nature of support among family members. Each member can play a certain role in covering the areas of business that need attention.

The other side of the coin is that a family business may lack professionalism or not have a well-functioning system because of the close relationship among family members. It might not be possible to force a system to be applied in the same way as you might force it on employees who are not family. Also, family businesses can initiate conflicts that affect relationships and make communication uncomfortable. When you meet them later a holiday or other family occasion, the separation of professional and emotional aspects can be tough, but it works for many people.

Online Business. In this Information Age, online businesses have revolutionized the business world and disrupted many industries and companies in the marketplace. You can start an online business focused on selling your products, or other people's products, as an affiliate and earn a commission. E-commerce concepts have revolutionized how business is done; your store and transactions are all done online. Many offline businesses have realized that they must sell their products online to get a share of the online pie. Online businesses have affected offline industries in a big way.

Look at what Amazon has done to normal retailers. Online businesses can be run in many ways and through many different channels:

- Websites or blogs
- E-commerce sites
- Forums and social media sites
- Network marketing and affiliate marketing sites
- Email marketing
- Outsourcing and virtual assistant services
- Design services via Upwork, Fiverr, 99Designs
- Membership sites
- Web TV Shows and webinars
- Hosting services
- Copywriting, translation or transcription services
- Programming, consulting and financial services
- Educational products, e-books, audio books

Online companies that involve physical products tend to be larger and more complicated, especially if they sell many different products.

The online world is becoming very competitive. If you want to start a small online business, you need to be unique and target a certain niche. You need to be aware of how you're going to market your idea online, have some technical skills, or have a technical co-founder to help you take care of those issues and hire the best technical assistance.

Allocate one to two hours a day to investigate the business you want to start online. Then test it. An online business will give you a greater amount of freedom, flexibility, efficiency, and scalability if you do your homework and set the business on the right path.

You must be patient and persistent. Learn, adapt and take action — fast. Technology is changing every day.

Independent Contractor. You can start a business as an independent contractor to provide a service, whether you focus on carpentry, cleaning or other skilled service. You can be self-employed in this category if you have a degree. An example is starting a clinic as a dentist. The basic problem with this type of business is that you must be there all the time. When you stop working, the money stops coming. It's not the ideal type of business to create passive income and become financially free, but this type of business gives you control over your destiny more than having a job. So it's fine to use it to generate money. If you're a dentist, you can buy or build a clinic that employs other dentists, providing them with a certain salary or commission. You generate passive income from the clinic instead of exchanging your time for money. The same thing applies to independent contractors on the Internet, such as virtual assistants, designers or translators.

Franchise Business. I like franchises; each is a ready-made business. You don't need excellent experience in business to run one, because you'll be given a working model and concept to operate, and all the necessary training to run the business so you don't need to struggle to invent a new concept and test whether it's going to work. You're going to continue and expand an already working concept, but you need to be careful when you select a franchise concept because not all of them work where you want to start one. Plus, most franchise businesses just want to sell you the license, get their franchise fee and collect royalties for a certain period of time, without necessarily caring whether your branch is going to work.

After you get a license, you need to study the franchiser's principles and be willing to follow its orders and apply them; otherwise, they'll pull the license from you. If you're someone who's good at following orders, go for it. If you like to do things your own way, start your own business, but I always recommend franchise businesses; in the right location, they work. A downside that prevents some people from taking the franchise route is that they are costly, especially the big brands, which demand a large franchise fee for the concept. The giants even require a certain amount of security money in the bank, to make sure you have the money to back up the concept for a certain amount of time.

It's best to start with a mid-range, well-known franchise brand instead of a first-line brand, because they are much more affordable. Choose brands that you want to open in new places. Franchisers might give you a better deal because they want to expand to new areas. Even if you pay a bit more for a franchise business, it will save you a lot of money and time along the way with more of a guarantee for success than starting your own business. If you Google franchise businesses on the Internet, you'll find many sites that specialize in promoting a variety of concepts. Some of them provide online life training and educational franchises; most are offline and range from restaurants to vending machines.

You can choose many franchise consultation companies to build a franchise business for you. Most of them are costly to build because they include an operational manual, legal contracts, and a strategy and marketing plan. This might cost you from $30,000 to $100,000 to go with a well-known franchise consulting company. Another less expensive way is to hire an individual franchise consultant. Those consultants charge way less, and you can probably pay them by the month to build on your knowledge. You can outsource some of your manuals to be done online via Upwork from other people who've done such manuals before, and who've worked in the franchise industry. This can cost you from $3,000 to $10,000 for the manuals if you do them online, but you still need to work with a consultant to put things together. There are many online who are willing and able to travel to check your business, advise you how to document it properly, and build its systems as a franchise.

License A Product or Service. You don't necessarily have to build a business; you can invent a product or specific service and license it to some big players in the market and collect royalties for your licensed idea. This works best with patented products or services. You need to have something unique and make sure that you patent it before it's copied. In some counties, the patent and legal costs are high and take time, but worthwhile if you have something special.

When you patent a product or service you must publicly state in the patent what's unique about it in terms of process or ingredients. Some companies steal the ingredients of patented products and come up with slightly different formulas, then also patent their copy and enter the market with it. If you're an inventor and not a businessperson, better focus on getting familiar with the licensing world. Work on licensing your products.

What's Your Passion?

The first thing you need to do before starting a business is to know who you are, your strengths and weaknesses; whether you're good at sales, technology, and/or accounting. What's your passion? Which industries do you like best? What things in life interest you the most? Is there a problem you've uncovered that you're passionate about finding a solution for?

Get Familiar with Your Real Skills

The essential things for efficient entrepreneurship is to be able to raise capital, sell, delegate and know how to leverage and scale a business you feel passionate about. Most of us don't have all these skills, but we can learn them over time from different resources, from our experience working in some fields, or by getting a partner or co-founder who can add value in the areas we don't know.

First a Feasibility Study, Then a Business Plan

The main difference between a feasibility study and a business plan is that a feasibility study is done before starting a business, to know whether it's feasible to pursue as a business venture before investing in the business. It helps you determine whether your idea is worth pursuing and likely to succeed.

A business plan is usually done after finding that a business opportunity exists and the venture is about to start. A feasibility study is a planning tool that includes financial projections. A business plan is more detailed in terms of numbers, strategies and tactics to run the business in terms of management, marketing and other important aspects. To raise capital from investors you need to have a business plan to illustrate the business's potential growth and profits, the market size, your likely customers, and how you're going to market and sell your products or services.

- *Feasibility Elements:* Financials, system, technology, market, legal operations, technical aspects and project scope.
- *Business Plan Elements:* Executive summary, company overview, market size, industry analysis, customer analysis, competitor analysis, business model, product analysis, growth potential, financial projection for three to five years, executive ownership, partners or key leadership team, management and human resources, operation overview, risk management, marketing overview, exit strategy, non-disclosure agreement.

These details can vary based on the size and kind of business. You can outsource these studies by using Upwork if you help them gather details about your business.

Know Your Budget

You can't start a business that costs $1 million dollars if you have only $1,000 in the bank and want to start a business on your own. You need to know your budget and financial capabilities to select the right business to start.

If you don't have enough money but want to start "the next big startup" and need a large amount of money, build a presentation pitch for your idea and try to get accepted by one of the startup incubators or accelerators to help you get some small financing at the beginning, shape your concept, build on your concept, practice how to pitch it to other investors, and in most cases put you in front of investors to pitch.

You need to also know your personal budget and how much you'll need to live if you decide to go full time with the business, expecting no investor involvement. This will help you understand how much time you must survive before going full time. If you can't go full time, you can opt to stay at your job and start with a small online idea.

Brand Your Concept and Choose an Entity

Think about your concept in terms of selecting the right name for your brand, making sure that the domain of the name you want to go with is available. If it is, buy the domain before making the final decision about the name of the brand. It's best to select an easy name to remember for the brand. Try your best to make it one or two words maximum.

Send company emails from the domain you've purchased so you appear professional when you communicate with other companies and customers. This is another activity you can outsource on Upwork. Or you can use a Gmail address if you don't want to use an email with your domain name.

Design the right logo and stationery for the brand for business cards, letterheads and flyers so that you properly stand out from the crowd and look professional. You can use 99designs, Upwork or Fivver.

Hire an Accountant

As you know by now, knowing your numbers well is a must, but you can't do it yourself forever. You need to track them and make decisions based on improving them. Doing the accounting on a daily basis can get challenging, boring, and time-consuming, so you might want to hire a full-time accountant for $500 to $3000, or outsource the accounting work, which can range from $200 to $700 a month, based on the volume of work there would be for your small business.

Choose the Right Business Entity

Choosing the right business entity is critical before starting your business. If you change it later, it will cost you a lot of money. Plus, choosing the right entity prevents you from many legal issues you'll want to avoid in the future. Spend some time learning the right entity for your business and consult a lawyer before choosing it.

These were mentioned earlier, but here they are in more detail. The common ones are:

Sole Proprietorship: This involves a single owner for the company — easy to form, easy to close, and common to use because of its complete managerial control by the sole owner. It's difficult to raise capital with this form since investors don't prefer it, and it will need to be changed to involve investors. Avoid this kind of entity as much as you can because it makes you financially liable on a personal level, which is a huge risk in case the business doesn't work or you face any legal challenges.

Partnership: This involves two or more partners in the company. Partners are liable personally for any financial losses based on the partnership type. There are two kinds: general partnership and limited partnership. In the general format, the partners are liable financially. In the limited form, the partners are not.

Corporation: The point of this kind of arrangement is to separate the financial business risk from the founding partners, to clear their financial responsibility. This arrangement is costly to form. There's double taxation with a corporation (C), first with taxes on profits, and second with taxes on stockholder dividends (capital gains). There's another form called an S-corporation, created to provide small corporations with the tax advantage of avoiding the double taxation on a regular corporation.

Limited Liability Company (LLC): This is common and highly recommended for most companies. The benefit of this entity is that it clears partners from financial risk, so in case of business loss, it will not be covered with your personal money or money from other companies you're involved in. An LLC is a mix between a partnership and a corporation, and is like a limited partnership but has some legal differences, which is why it's best to consult an attorney to see what works best. There's far less paperwork involved in creating an LLC than a corporation.

Each industry has its own unique legal, operational and business requirements. Choose what you understand more and what you are passionate about most. Don't let people talk you into starting a business or investing in a certain venture that doesn't excite you. Do what you understand and know, not what others would like you to do. The more knowledge you have, the better your choices will be. You must educate yourself financially. Some experts will help you in certain areas, but you need to guide the ship and know what to invest in. All experts have their own opinions, based on their skills, background and circumstances. There are general rules for investing and different areas to invest in, but you need to get yourself educated and then choose what you feel works best for you. Every industry or investment has its advantages and disadvantages. Nothing is perfect. Keep learning.

Take Action

There is never a perfect time to make the transition from employee to entrepreneur and start a business. There's always risk involved and other factors that can discourage you. Some times may be better than other times, but you need to take action regardless of any criticism around you — and just do it. If you want advice, remember to take it only from people who've done what you want to do.

All the planning in the world will never be perfect to start a business. There will always something missing that you didn't have time for, money or other resources to acquire; but you need to start somewhere. Action and execution make up more than 95% of the success of most businesses. Ideas on paper don't matter more than 2% to 5% compared with action. Experience will teach you the most; failure will teach you more than success. You can't calculate anything 100% to guarantee success, so just do the best you can — and go for it.

I wish from the bottom of my heart that you'll find an endless amount of fulfillment, happiness and success, and that you'll share it with me one day and tell me you made it.

Finding Money

The world today has no lack of ideas but rather lack of speed in implementation. Some of it arises from not knowing how to raise money. TV shows like "Shark Tank" have been instructive, as has the Silicon Valley startup movement, which has reached most parts of the world.

Learn how to use your credit card to open small projects. You can also learn about angel investors, venture capital, incubators and crowd funding. Investors are available but the primary question is, once you find them, how to convince them of your big dream idea. Thanks to the Internet, finding investors has become easier, as has finding events to attend.

Investors are looking for something that makes them more money. Once they're convinced that your idea is going to do that, and you're qualified enough to help them do that, they will give you their money and many of them will support you at a variety of levels.

Raising capital is learnable. It's not easy when you start, but the more you focus, the more you insist, the more you go on and believe in yourself and keep trying, you're going to get there.

Acting on something will lead you to a result. If it doesn't turn out well, then you're at least going to learn a lot. As already discussed, negative results are what you learn from the most, because you never forget your mistakes. Measure and manage your risk so that you can come back wiser.

Start small, think big. Begin with a project that costs less than $10,000, $100,000 at the most, not more than that, to begin to learn from it and come back faster if you fail.

The offline world tends to cost more money, but there are some ideas that cost less than $10,000 to $30000. Many online ideas cost less than that to start. Many of them cost less than even $5,000 if we're talking about an app or something you can build or outsource to start lean then market slowly. So, you have more chances to try and correct, fail and correct, adjust and improve — until you break through.

Take action. Motivate yourself, and spend time with people who can motivate you. Understand that failing is a normal thing and part of the success formula. Even after you have succeeded with ten projects, you can still fail.

The most important thing is to be able to cover your basic expenses. Even if you live below your means for a couple of months, or years, if you have a big plan, you can benefit and break through, which is better than living your entire life below your means because you don't want to take a risk. I can assure you that not taking any risk is the worst plan ever, because if you don't, you will never gain the knowledge and experience you need to win.

Select the Right Location

Locating in a Mall

I managed to close many deals with the leasing department of many different malls, and I'm still learning more about the process — how to negotiate and close a deal with a leasing department in a mall. The process includes politics and continual and consistent follow-up as well as certain techniques to break through mall management and close the deal.

Selecting the right location for your brand, as a business owner, is one of the most important things you must do, especially if you're setting up in a mall. Typically, malls are filled with lots of brands, some of which include competitors, irrelevant brands to your niche, and those that are complementary to your brand. Finding the right location requires careful thought. The following are some simple things to consider.

One of the most important questions to ask yourself is: Will my brand fit in this mall? To answer this question, you'll have to conduct your research beforehand to determine the kind of competition that exists in the mall, or lack thereof. The size of the mall is also important, whether it's large or small. Is the mall famous or not? Is the mall located in a tourist city?

Though not all mall management departments can do this, you can attempt to inquire into the periodic visitor traffic in the mall. If possible, take your time and visit other malls so you have an idea of what they're offering compared to the one you're interested in. Generally, a mall worth your time should have at least 10,000 to 40,000 visitors a day.

Before you get space in a mall, the management will usually ask you for a presentation of your business or company. In the process, you might have some forms to fill out regarding the space you want and any other details management might find necessary.

Once you've filled out the forms expected, you'll wait for management to contact you. In most cases, they never do, but this does not mean you should give up. If you get a quick response, chances are high that: Your brand is successful and well-known; they are struggling; or, your presentation was awesome; your brand is a perfect fit for a specific location at the mall; you have an insider.

Conducting Needed Research

In order for you not to be overwhelmed by the process, it's advisable that you hire someone whose role would be to look through the prospective malls you're interested in to save you time.

Don't get too excited about the mall because this might influence the owner's options out of your favor. You should be aware that getting the location right does not always happen to everyone, and the reality is that there are those who've managed to get stores in high traffic malls but still have not managed to break even. The rent, footfall, and visitor demographics are all factors that participate directly to the success of your brand at any mall.

Researching Demographics

Getting the demographics of the mall is an important element. You'll want to know the type of clientele you'll be dealing with. From ages to nationalities, this is important. You can extend this knowledge to finding out the particulars of those who live around the mall, their age groups, the things they like, their cultural affiliations.

Exploring the Competition

Competition is always the key to your brand location. There are brands that will thrive from the economies associated with their competitors, especially in the technology sector. However, this does not work for all businesses. Depending on how you want to work your brand, proximity to your competitors can work both ways. Unsatisfied competitor customers can seek solace with your brand, while you might lose some to the competition. This is a tricky affair, but an important element to take into consideration.

Proximity and Accessibility

One thing that you can be guaranteed is that a mall is usually a crowded place, full of stores and people. Therefore, you need to determine how easy it will be to access your brand for your target buyers. All brand owners want to have their stores easily accessible to shoppers. The easier it is for clients to access your store, the easier it will be for you to do business. Most shoppers prefer stores where they can walk in and out conveniently without feeling claustrophobic.

Future Growth

Is there room for growth for your brand at the mall? This is an important question if you're planning to expand the brand over the coming trading periods. You'll want an appropriate location that allows you the kind of flexibility you need.

Costs

Chances are high that the spot you'll get will not be business ready. Therefore, you'll need to consider possible renovation costs, decoration, IT system installation and upgrades. Consider whether you can afford such costs comfortably while handling the requirements for setting up your brand.

Eventually the right location for your business will come down to how much you're willing to pay to lease it. You must conduct enough research about the mall, the potential for growth, the owner's perception of your line of business and other aspects that determine the amount of money you'll be required to spend for your ideal space.

Negotiating a Deal with the Leasing Department

Before you set out to get a lease for your shop or kiosk from a mall, there are a number of things you have to get right to be sure of a good deal with respect to your lease agreement. Doing so will safeguard you from lease details being misunderstood.

Most malls set their rent per square foot or meter, so it's important to ask about this beforehand. Ask whether there's a service charges involved in getting the lease and, if possible, whether the mall operators provide air conditioning free or your contract states that it's part of the utility bill.

If the mall hasn't yet opened, find out the opening policy of the mall. Some malls open with 50% to 70% of stores occupied, while others start operation with only 30% to 40% and later replace stores that are failing. Take some time to consider the track record of the company managing the mall — its operation history and how it handles clients. Not all malls are the same. Some can take up to a year to pick up traffic, while others can take up to three.

Take time to speak with your store neighbors and find out how much they pay for their service and utility bills, and any other costs they incur to do business. Are there any expected brands that might rival or complement your brand? Look at the entrances and the gates to determine whether they're suitable.

As you enter into contract negotiations, consider the length of the lease — when the lease expires. There are mall owners who demand in their agreement that you completely renovate the store after your contract expires. This can eat up your profits. Also find out if and how much the rent will be increasing per year. Some malls have their own companies that take care of repairs and maintenance work inside the mall. The costs involved can be higher than what would be incurred if you hired your own contractors.

Most malls will set different rates depending on the time of year you intend to open your store. Say, for example, that you're dealing in toys, November and December would be ideal months for you, but remember that, no matter your products or services, you need at least 6 to 12 months' budget to be able to survive the challenges involved after you open your store.

Look into the terms and conditions before you sign any document. The pages might be long and boring, but there's a reason for that. If you can't do it, get your legal advisor to take you through them one by one before you commit. There are some that will require a security deposit, while others will want a profit or revenue sharing agreement. Also, consider if there are controlled standards in place for making any renovations in the mall.

The nature of your merchandise will determine the type of the lease you are getting, and if the mall in question is suitable for you. Talk with either the mall owner, the General Manager, Leasing Manager or whoever can get you as close as possible to getting a good deal, and who can help you understand the contract details.

It's important for you to negotiate a number of free months within which you'll be carrying out some repairs, setting up your infrastructure and other structures in the mall. Be very keen on this because most malls offer it but only if you ask for it. Therefore, if you move in and start setting up, you won't need to start paying rent immediately. If you plan to make any changes or do any construction work during the free months, be sure to inform the management if these will require some approval from external authorities. This is important so that you don't have to start paying for time while there's a delay in the approval process.

The termination policy is also an important factor to consider. If you're to terminate the contract before it expires naturally, would there be a penalty, and how much would it be? Knowing about this will help you limit your liability. Consider the installation of the heating, ventilation and air conditioning (HVAC) systems, and whether they're centralized, or if you're supposed to install yours on your own. Also, find out whether there are enough parking spaces, not just for your clients, but also for your employees, if possible.

You can negotiate with mall owners the nature of the rent agreement once the contract expires. Will they increase the rent, and if so, by how much? This is important if you intend to stay in the mall for another lease period. The other thing to remember is to find out if there is a penalty for not opening your store on the agreed time. If this exists, try to negotiate to shift the date later or to remove the clause altogether in the event that you're not sure about when you'll open. This is because in most cases the penalty is always more than you would pay for rent.

CHAPTER 9

THE ART OF EFFICIENCY

"Don't be fooled by the calendar. There are only as many days in the year as you make use of. One man gets only a week's value out of a year while another man gets a full year's value out of a week."
— *Charles Richards*

Now that you've thought about your career, improved your financial literacy, created a vision and set a path toward learning all you can, here are some tips on making your business and life as efficient as it can be.

An App That Can Help You Budget Wisely

If you want to run a well-organized business and grow your money, you need to invest in multiple sources of income, especially sources that work for you without exchanging your time for money. As we've discussed, you can begin by investing 10% of your income and, over time, you'll grow financially by eventually investing 90% while only spending 10% of your income. This is because your income will increase, and you'll no longer need most it for living.

Most middle-class people today live on an amount between $1,000 and $10,000 per month. Regardless of how much money you make, it's important to budget your money.

People who experience financial problems simply don't know how to budget expenses wisely. While most know how much they're making, many don't know how much they're spending. Creating a budget is an absolute must if you want to take control of your expenses, pay down your debts, grow financially, and invest more wisely.

I use a paid app called Home Budget on my iPhone to plug in all my expenses. Whether I'm buying movie tickets, paying the check at a restaurant, or spending money on anything else, I log in and enter the expense.

This app allows you to create different accounts. For instance, you can create accounts for your credit cards, personal accounts, investment accounts, and more. When you spend money, you simply enter the expense in the account used for the expenditure. If you're spending money on behalf of your business, you can input that separately, so you don't forget how much you've paid on behalf of your company. The app will show you the balance in each account or on each credit card and provide you with a clear understanding of your personal and business financial situation.

Home Budget is easy to use. You can plug whatever amount you spend into the proper category, or input income you've received into any of your accounts. There's a calculator to assist you, which can be helpful for exchange rates. When you pull up the app to enter an amount, it automatically defaults to the current date. Simply select the correct category and the account, then input your data. You also can add notes about each expense which makes it easy to remember certain purchases. Plus, you can view and compare different monthly reports to track your financial performance and cash-flow.

The app also allows you to split expenses. Let's say you want to pay three months' rent in advance, and you want to divide the expense over those three months for budgeting purposes. The Home Budget app will split the expense for you. It has a section for bills you can place on the calendar and pay from the correct accounts automatically. You can also enter a due date for each bill, such as your credit cards, so you know when those payments need to be made. There's another section where you can enter income when it's received or make it automatic, which can be helpful if you have payments that come in automatically. It will also allow you to enter cash as income.

One of the best features of this app is that you can see, over time, how much income you have—and how much you've spent. The Target Budget section of the app allows you to budget monthly for certain expenses and then confirm how much you have left to spend.

You can have a cash account and investment account — and shift money between them. If you need to do so, it will also allow you to export your expenses into an Excel spreadsheet.

Another helpful feature is the ability to create a list of payees. The app also allows you to review reports for different months and even search for certain expenses. One of the ways I use this app is to track my bank accounts, especially my business accounts, so I know at all times how much money I have to pay my expected bills.

Home Budget allows me to merge my entire financial system, understand how to schedule cash flow, and stay on track with my budget. I highly recommend this app, particularly for anyone who wants to be more financially organized.

Get Familiar with Parking Alternatives

Weekends are the busiest time of the week for shopping malls and you can often drive around the parking lot multiple times looking for an available spot. Not only is this frustrating, but it also wastes your time.

While this may not apply to certain areas of the world, many of the larger malls in Dubai, where I live, have hotels attached. I park in the hotel valet parking and stop by one of the restaurants at the hotel to eat lunch or dinner. This way I avoid the crowded mall parking lot, and save time.

If the hotel restaurant you choose is expensive, you can order a salad or dessert to go on your way out and still get your valet parking ticket stamped, also for overtime. I've developed relationships with many of the staff in the restaurants I visit, and eventually they gave me cards to use for valet parking, instead of giving me one card per visit as normally allowed. By receiving 10-20 cards per visit, I can turn one visit to the restaurant into free, convenient parking for the next few months. I use this secret weapon often, especially on crowded weekends.

You can also use this method when you attend exhibitions as there are usually hotels attached to a convention center.

Why You Should Lead a TV-Free Life

While many people spend significant amounts of time today watching television, it's been about five years since I stopped. I first decided to stop watching the news because it seemed there was always something bad going on and it was depressing. Later, I discovered that many productive people share the same habit of not watching television.

Eventually, I did decide to buy a TV — a really large one — after I moved into my new flat three years ago, but I opted not to have cable service hooked up. Now, I mirror the screen of my Mac or iPhone through Apple TV to watch online courses, movies or some entertainment shows just to relax for an hour or two per day. While it can be argued that I still watch TV, the difference is that I'm very choosy about what I watch.

The question of whether to watch television or not is really one of time-consumption versus entertainment. There is certainly nothing wrong with taking a break during the day to get away from work and relax. Everyone needs to take a break. But not having cable service has allowed me to watch directly whatever interests me--at the time I choose—with no commercials (and less cost).

I never have to wait for something to come on that I want to watch and never waste time flipping through channels searching for what I want to see.

Still, for any entrepreneur, watching television can be extremely addicting. It eventually kills your productivity and creativity. You think less for yourself and grow less happy. Some people will often say, "Well, I only watch something educational like Discovery Channel." That's not really the point. Television is designed to get you in the habit of watching many things you never intended to watch.

For me, it's been tremendously advantageous to simply stop watching. I am more productive and happier. I have found that watching less TV has made me more social, because it's given me more time to communicate with family and friends. I also get to spend more time on my health and exercise. You even eat less when you watch less TV. Spending vast amounts of time watching TV encourages you to continue putting something in your mouth. That's precisely what commercials are designed to do, make you want things.

The Importance of Having a "To Do" List

In today's hectic world we all struggle to get more done. While we're spending more and more time working, sometimes it seems that we're accomplishing less and less. What I've discovered is that the key to getting things done is having a To Do List. It's extremely important when you want to be more efficient and productive.

236 | The Efficientpreneur

To help me write and manage my list, I use an app called 2Do, available for MAC, iOS and Android. I recommend putting it on the homepage of your smartphone. If you use an iPhone, for instance, add it to the bottom fixed bar so that it's readily available and visible. You need to program yourself to use it and check it throughout the day to stay on track with what you need to accomplish.

With 2Do, you have a tremendous amount of functionality, such as the ability to prioritize each task based on a set level you assign to them. Additionally, you can sync it with your Mac computer so that everything is updated automatically.

2Do allows you to create checklists, projects, and perform a variety of other tasks. Most people use it to create task lists, but you can also use it to notate due dates for tasks, as well as assign certain actions for your task such as a text or phone call that needs to be made. This way, you'll always know what action needs to be taken for that particular task. You can even enter a time and a location so that you're reminded of upcoming events. Audio notes can be added, too.

What's best about this app is that you can add tabs based on what you want to accomplish. For instance, you might add a computer tab so that when you're at your computer, you can check in and see what you need to do. It's a good idea to create a work tab for general work, but you can also create tabs for your different business activities.

If you're out and about a lot, you might want to create a To Do list or tab for errands as well, so you don't forget to do a required activity while you're out. You can also create a "future projects" tab for things you want to accomplish down the road, such as books you want to read, places you want to go, and people you want to contact.

Another important use of this app is to create a call list for the people you need to contact. You might consider creating a home tab, where you can enter things you need to do for your home. This app will show you a list of items that are completed, so you always know what's been completed. There's also a main sidebar that shows all the tabs you've created—with different colors to distinguish them from each other. Shifting tasks to different categories is easily done. It's truly an amazing app.

Safely Store and Sync Your Data

The era of floppy disks, small hard drives, and losing data has come to an end. We used to have to send a hard drive to a professional to recover files after a mishap. Sometimes the data could be recovered, but in most cases, when systems failed, all would be lost.

Then hard disks began to get bigger. Later, the world of technology began producing external hard drives, continually making them larger as they developed over time. The problem with an external hard drive is that you must continually back up your data to ensure everything is safe. This is not efficient, especially with how the amount of data has been increasing.

This era of problematic data storage is over.

Dropbox now makes it possible to keep your data secure and be more productive, too. If you're not familiar with Dropbox, it's a free service that allows you to place all of your documents, data, photos, and videos in a "box" and share them easily by putting them in the Cloud (a model for delivering information technology services where resources are located on the Internet through web-based tools and applications rather than via a direct connection to a server). Basically, it acts as a hosting service for all your data. You can back it up and synch it continually.

In order to take advantage of these benefits, open an account with Dropbox that lets you save a certain amount of data free. You can create a folder on your computer, tablet, or smartphone. When you create your account, Dropbox creates a folder where you can store up to 2GB of information and automatically synch it to the Cloud. Whatever document or file you place in the folder will update automatically if you make changes to it on any of your other devices.

You also have the opportunity to invite others to join the service and earn free data storage. If people join Dropbox through your invitation, you receive 500MG per referral up to 16GB, so you're able to increase your data storage limit. You can also earn up to 1GB per friend if you're subscribed to the Pro account, up to 32GB. Dropbox also offers the ability to earn free storage if you connect via your social media pages or link your mailbox.

If you need more storage or can't convince friends to join, Dropbox has paid versions available, such as the Pro plan starting at $9.99 per month. They also provide a business plan that offers an unlimited amount of data.

Dropbox has a feature called Packrat that gives you unlimited deletion recovery and version history. By default, Dropbox saves a history of all deleted and earlier versions of your files for 30 days, so you don't have to live in fear that you or one of the people you've shared folders with deletes you're a file by mistake. You can contact Dropbox and they'll recover the file for you. If you purchase Packrat, you won't have to worry about losing a deleted folder or file because Dropbox will save your files for as long as you have the feature. As of this writing, Packrat is available to all Dropbox Pro accounts for $3.99 per month or $39.00 per year.

You can share links or folders with friends and team members; then, if necessary, you can change the link later or unshare the folder. Dropbox offers an unlimited deletion recovery service for an annual fee, a service to which I subscribe. And Dropbox makes it easy to access data from anywhere. For instance, if you attend a meeting and don't have your computer, you can access your data directly from the app on your smartphone. This can give you tremendous peace of mind and fast access to any document.

Use Task Management Tools

I work with both online and offline teams, and 99% of the time I manage both teams wirelessly from the comfort of my home. Today, the primary method of communication is email, along with other tools, but one of the biggest problems I experienced in managing my teams was sending emails and not getting a reply.

With all the emails you send, it can be difficult to keep track of who's doing what task, who has responded and what's taking place with each person. To combat this problem, I discovered a tool called Asana. It's a task management tool for teams. There are other similar task management software products available, but after conducting some research and viewing some videos, I've concluded that Asana is the best option available, by far.

One of Asana's best features is that you can use it on your computer or as an app on your smartphone. Basically, Asana allows you to create a project with an unlimited number of tasks. It's free, too, which is awesome.

With Asana, you can create multiple projects and name them. Inside each project, you can share information with certain members who are able to see the tasks you've created inside that project. In addition, you can create a description for each task and even assign deadlines. You also can assign a task to someone who'll be responsible for completing and delivering that task.

Asana even lets you assign followers who are able to see and contribute to each task. For instance, you can assign a task manager, but other people can contribute to the task. Whenever someone comments on the task, you'll be notified by email. When you add followers to the project, you do so via their email addresses, and they receive an invitation to use Asana. In this regard, everyone can comment, or mark tasks as complete or incomplete. This makes it incredibly easy for teams to accomplish projects while boosting productivity, regardless of the team size.

The above Asana dashboard shows projects, tasks and one task with its full description.

You have the option of assigning tasks to an assistant, but even if you don't have an assistant, this tool is worthwhile to use just for yourself. You can download the app on your smartphone. Simply create a task and share with the people you want, and then you can track what's happening with that task. You can even come back a few days or a week later to evaluate progress, establish deadlines, comments, and reminders. Nothing is ever deleted. Everything is documented.

Asana can be integrated easily with other tools such as Chrome Extension, DropBox, Google Drive, WordPress, Evernote, Mailchimp, Wufoo, Calendar Sync, and Weekdone to make things easier. If you haven't already considered these, all of them are worth exploring.

With this one great tool, you can be more productive and ensure that you never have to worry again about your team ignoring your emails, plus it's better for archiving than emails. Now I communicate with my team mainly through Asana.

Make Emailing Ten Times More Efficient

Email is effective because it's:

- Universal – everyone has it
- An important way to communicate with team and customers
- More efficient than writing or sending letters
- Inexpensive and time-saving
- Easy to send to more than one person at a time
- Quick, accurate, private and a reliable form of information
- Good for recordkeeping and archiving
- Got attachment capability and delivery confirmation

Since I shifted managing my business from offline to online, I've been searching for and testing new ways of managing one of the greatest wastes of time I've encountered during my transition: my email inbox. The system I'm currently using (AKemail) took me two years to perfect.

While fewer than 10% of my businesses are online, and the remaining 90% are offline, I manage some of my communication with my investors, partners, franchisees, branch managers, personal assistant, as well as my online team of accountants, researchers, web developers, graphic designers, lawyers, transcribers and social media managers, primarily via email.

I receive around 200 to 300 emails a day from maybe 50 people offline (10 direct connections), employees offline (10 direct connections), 150 people online (15 direct connections), about 15 direct partners and investors, daily partnership and joint venture proposals; plus friends and family, email subscriptions, social media, and spam.

This model allows me to avoid having an office and specific working hours, and to wake up anytime I want, work from anywhere I want, travel anytime, play my favorite sport anytime, and more importantly, have free time to spend with people I want to spend it with.

The most challenging thing I've faced after shifting to this online management style is the tsunami of emails I receive. Just checking and replying to these emails was taking me 6 to 12 hours a day. In effect, I had created another full-time job for myself, which required sitting in front of the computer and replying to emails. In theory, it's not a bad job compared to what other people might do, because I can still do it from the beach, the mall, a café, or home, and I can do it in stages — not necessarily all at once. But still, it was taking over my brain and my life, simply because it took so much time.

The step-by-step process I now use to send and reply to emails takes 95% less time than before. Here's some advice.

242 | The Efficientpreneur

Hire a Virtual Assistant to Handle Your Emails

You can hire a VA through Upwork.com on an hourly basis. This will cost you from $4 to $10 an hour. I currently pay about $6 an hour to my VA, at a monthly cost of $150 to $200. Bear in mind that this virtual assistant will have access to your emails, so select this person wisely and test him or her with a less important email account before providing access to your main email accounts.

Your VA can read your emails and send them to you as voice messages through WhatsApp on your mobile device in the following format:

Text from VA: Email: (As per the sequence of emails received that day) (Sender, Name) (Subject)

Voice from VA: This is a recording of the email received, which should always start with the email number to avoid confusion if you've sent them a message via WhatsApp in the meantime.

Text from You: (Email number)

Voice from You: (Your voice replies to the email)

Text from You: (Your written answer, in case you prefer to reply in writing)

For personal emails that only you must reply to, or those critical to a business deal, or financial statements, or emails from high profile people, or those that might include an attachment you need to review, you need to reply to your VA's voice message as follows:

Voice Message from VA

Text from You: (Email number, (F) which stands for forward, but forward to where?

You need to create a secret email address that nobody knows about except for your VA. Even your family and friends should not know about this email address, because this is where your VA will forward emails you need to review or reply to on your own.

This means that now you'll have three to five emails to check daily at your secret email address (and no spam!) instead of having to check 100 to 200 in your main inbox. Your VA will act as a gatekeeper as well as a quick answering and forwarding machine between you and the world.

Depending on the type of email reply you want to send, your VA can reply from his or her email address and use a range of business cards when replying on your behalf, so your reply appears to come directly from you.

When I want to send an email to my team or reply to the emails at my secret email address, I use a free app called Say It & Mail It, because when you speak, you usually deliver the idea you want in a better and faster way, plus you avoid having to use a formal greeting, needing to proofread for spelling mistakes, or continually reviewing your written response.

Asana

I discovered recently that by combining Asana with this powerful email checking system, your system becomes even more powerful. You can use Asana primarily for communication with your team members, with such items as financial statements that you need to see, review and provide input for — or an urgent project design you need to review. Asana is good to use for expected information from your team, such as search engine optimization (SEO), design, email marketing, accounting and any other materials you want to review. Both expected and unexpected emails can involve important/unimportant and urgent/not urgent information, but most of the time the most important items are those you're working on with your team.

The point of separation from some emails between the Whatsapp system and Asana is to focus on what's most important, make the process of checking emails less important to you because it's not proactive, and save you time.

Mistakes can happen sometimes, but in terms of efficiency it's the best system I've found. Now I spend about 15 to 30 minutes a day answering emails, unless one of them includes something like a partnership agreement or leasing contract that needs more attention. On Asana, I spend about 15 to 45 minutes.

Finding the right tools can be overwhelming. There are so many choices that it can be hard to find the right tools to meet your needs. I have put together a list of the tools that I have personally used to build my business. Go to www.ahmedalkiremli.com/tools to get the complete list of my tools.

Finally, your virtual assistant—based on your instructions—can do some research related to the emails you receive. You can ask your VA to opt-out for you on ongoing newsletters you may have registered for but no longer have an interest in receiving. Your VA can contact people for you, if needed, and provide many other ways to help you be efficient when you begin to use Whatsapp.

It can be helpful to make a business card for your VA, as well as one for yourself. Then you can occasionally ask your VA to respond personally, and if a receiver has a problem with your VA's response, you can contact that person yourself, apologize for how something was handled, and make everything right. You'll want a copy of the VA's business card so you can use it yourself at times to show that you have a team answering on your behalf.

There are a multitude of ways to make yourself the most efficient you can possibly be. Explore what works best for you, and never stop learning how to improve.

"Entrepreneurship is living a few years of your life like most people won't, so that you can spend the rest of your life like most people can't."
— Anonymous

FINAL THOUGHTS

"Don't let the fear of losing be greater than the excitement of winning."
— Robert Kiyosaki

Remember that fulfillment is the goal and Efficientpreneurship is the path. Entrepreneurship is not an easy journey. At certain points in life or career, we all experience failure Maybe we fail in terms of business, career, or relationships with family and other people we love; but whatever the way, it's important to understand and accept that failure is part of the process, part of your career, your new business, part of whatever you're going to do. You should always approach it as an opportunity to learn.

As long as you believe that failure is part of the process of learning, you'll realize that it's best to look at it from that perspective. Regardless of how much you plan, how much you study your projects, how much you study your partner — there are going to be elements of failure. Those elements are what you can note and correct over time in the same venture or for your next venture.

When you're prepared for the possibility of failure, it will not take you 10 years to get back on your feet. It might take a year or two, depending on the project and how focused and persistent you are in terms of your actions. You may need more time to absorb new policies, new information. When you fail at something, usually you never forget it. You know not to repeat what didn't work, and always try to fix what went wrong.

246 | The Efficientpreneur

Failure Is Feedback in Disguise

To help you change your mindset around failure, think of it as feedback instead. And while it might take you some time to "practice" this new definition, realize that without failure you would not be the person you are today in terms of character, career and business ventures. Instead of seeing failure as something negative, think of it instead as new information you didn't have before. Use failure as a mentor. Learn from it, adjust your strategy or approach, and start again more efficiently.

Employees Gamble with Their Lives Long-Term, While Entrepreneurs Take Calculated Risks Short-Term

The beauty of entrepreneurship is the journey. And regardless of how difficult the journey, your sweat and tears will always pay off—maybe not instantly, but surely in the near future. The outcome is always determined by how persistent and focused you are toward your entrepreneurial goals.

When you fail in business, the lessons you learn will never go to waste. They may help you discover your passion. They may help you modify your next concept or refine your business model. Or maybe they will help you realize that you aren't in the right industry—and help you identify the right one for you.

Whatever lessons are yours to learn, never give up on your entrepreneurial dreams. If other have succeeded, you can, too—maybe achieving even more than they did. Believe in yourself. Stay focused and take action on your objectives.

Most People Fail Because They're More Committed to Their Comfort Than They Are to Their Mission

Start small and think big by having a long-term vision. Employees seek comfort. They prefer to be happy in the short-term with a consistent paycheck, but unfortunately, they also usually struggle their entire lives. Entrepreneurs, on the other hand, prefer to be stressed and under pressure for a short period of, say, one to five years—so that they can enjoy time freedom and financial freedom for the rest of their lives.

"Twenty years from now, you will be more disappointed by the things that you didn't do than by the ones you did do. So throw off the bowlines. Sail away from the safe harbor. Catch the trade winds in your sails. Explore. Dream. Discover."
—Mark Twain

Start today. If you're still employed, start thinking about something to work on. Observe the problems around you. To get an idea of whether a particular problem could be the start of a business venture for you, investigate how widespread the problem is—then measure the size of the potential market for a solution to that problem. The bigger the problem, the more golden an opportunity it may be for you to start your business.

Work on your new venture on the weekend or dedicate a couple of hours a day to it. Create some deadlines for benchmark goals, then adjust them based on your research, findings, mentor's input, and any challenges you expect to face. It might take you up to five years to achieve your entrepreneurial goal, but if you don't take action, nothing about your life will change—and your dream of financial freedom will be just that...a dream. Only action can turn those dreams into a reality.

Simply by implementing the concepts in this book, you'll achieve your goals. And you'll probably surprise yourself at the exceptional speed with which you do. Believe in yourself, create a plan for pursuing your entrepreneurial dream, then take focused action to achieve it.

And don't forget: Never stop learning—before, during and even after your entrepreneurial journey is finished. Once we stop learning, we diminish in spirit and in purpose, so keep improving your knowledge to add value to mankind and leave a legacy by which the world will remember you.

Finally, I wish you all the best in your entrepreneurial endeavors, I hope to hear from you about your entrepreneurial journey with all its ups and downs, please share it with me on any of my social media platforms or by emailing me on ahmed@ahmedalkiremli.com.

This book is just the beginning. Entrepreneurship is a changing landscape. Join me as I share book updates and cutting edge techniques at AKTips.com

THANK YOU FOR
READING THIS BOOK

In an industry where everybody seems to be making bigger and bigger promises…

YOU'VE made the biggest promise possible – to yourself.

According to statistics, only 15% of people who buy books like this one read it all the way to the end. If you're reading this, it means you've got serious willpower and a commitment to your future.

The only thing left now is to IMPLEMENT these tools and create the success you deserve.

In order to make that as easy as possible, I've taken my time out of my work schedule to prepare a little "secret sauce" for you to make that road a little easier. I'm VERY proud of the work I've put into it, and I know you'll be quite pleased with it from minute one.

Just go to www.ahmedalkiremli.com/book and register for it. Once you have it, I think you'll feel like a kid on Christmas, and you'll really understand how much I treasure having you on this journey with me.

When you register, you'll also get a free subscription to my newsletter, built from the ground up to give you encouragement, motivation, and up-to-date discoveries. That means you're not left wondering whether something works right now – I'm not going to put it in front of you unless it works TODAY.

Before you do that though, I'd like to ask you for a favor. Nowadays, a single review can have a massive impact on the success of a book. So head to Amazon.com and leave an honest review of this book. It'll help me immensely, and help everyone else considering a read.

To Your Success,
Ahmed

ABOUT THE AUTHOR

Ahmed Al Kiremli is a serial entrepreneur, franchisor, business strategist, efficiency expert, author and television personality.

He created the first-ever Iraqi franchise, Games Corner, which became the #1 video-gaming brand at malls. Additionally, he founded the world's first Iraqi food franchise and catering brand, Iraqi Touch. In the retail market, he developed the Kids Soft Play and Entertainment brand (visit ClimbAndSlide.com). And he is the developer of Movie Ratings App (visit BestMovieRatings.com), enabling moviegoers to read movie information before spending time and money. He has also invested in a wide range of successful startup ventures.

He is most widely known, however, as the host of Be Efficient Tv, a television show that helps viewers increase their productivity—in life and business—with tips from leading experts. His blog on the subjects of business and efficiency can be found at AhmedAlKiremli.com.

As a popular television personality, Mr. Al Kiremli is also in high demand as a speaker and has inspired tens of thousands of business owners at conferences, seminars, corporate events and workshops—including such large-scale events as TEDx, Elance and FailCon. His topics include entrepreneurship, efficiency, life-work balance, personal finance, sales, marketing, branding, social media, outsourcing and time management.

A major topic for his audiences is "How to Be 10x More Efficient" in their business and home life using a minimum amount of time, effort and cost. He shows audiences how to acquire and leverage new skills, how to seek out opportunities, and how to balance work and their private lives. He has worked in numerous industries including food and beverage, gaming, construction materials, power generators, the technology sector, stationery and office supplies, the advertising field, giftware, and transportation services—teaching leading companies and their employees.

He holds a Bachelor of Science degree in Biology from the University of Baghdad (Iraq) and an MBA from the University of Phoenix (United States).

In his personal quest for lifelong learning and knowledge, Mr. Al Kiremli has read countless books and worked with numerous mentors—developing a unique approach to work-life balance and business success that he now teaches to others as a corporate strategist and expert on entrepreneurship. Through a combination of outsourcing and productive delegation, Mr. Al Kiremli has achieved the coveted goal of all entrepreneurs: free time to pursue the projects and new opportunities of his choice. Using specific methodologies he has developed, he now manages his many business ventures and investment projects from home or from anywhere in the world.

Mr. Al Kiremli is an avid athlete and was Iraqi's #1 Squash player for seven years—playing an astonishing 10 seasons for the National Team and earning more money from his Squash career than from both his university degrees. He currently plays Squash in the PSA World Tour and the Dubai League, as well as in various local and international tournaments. Visit SquashInDubai.com for details about his Squash career and coaching activities. An advocate of adding sports as a continuous interest and different dimension to one's life, from age 7 to 24 years—throughout school and university—Mr. Al Kiremli played and captained teams in many different sports ranging from soccer, basketball, and badminton to ping pong, handball and volleyball.

As a lifelong entrepreneur, Mr. Al Kiremli has a lengthy history of success dating back to his youth, including numerous early forays into business. His earliest venture—at age 6—occurred at school where he sold sheets of stickers to earn money for snacks and sweets after his parents cut his allowance money.

By age 22, he had become a key supplier of computers, electronics and DVDs to an Iraqi retail chain—making the equivalent of US$50,000 in just four months. He credits his early sales and communications skills as an essential part of this success. That same year, Mr. Al Kiremli learned the difficult lesson of trust, as he rescued a friend from debt by investing in a computer shop the friend owned. Trusting the friend to make a success of the shop and repay the debt, Mr. Al Kiremli instead saw the business fail due to mismanagement and dishonesty. "Learn and move on" was the lesson Mr. Al Kiremli took from that early investment experience.

He eventually founded the leading computer retailer and DVD rental location in Iraq—developing a remarkable design and choosing a key location. As the success of the business grew, Mr. Al Kiremli branched out into importing computer goods from Dubai and China. Unfortunately, the advent of the Iraqi civil war in 2005 not only compelled Mr. Al Kiremli to leave Iraq, it took its toll on the business, as he was unable to manage the operations remotely. Still, he took his knowledge of retailing, wholesale businesses, import-export, team development and inventory management from this venture to later ones.

At age 25, he relocated to Dubai—discovering a brand-new world of potential. Seeing an opportunity to compete with and become the best in the world of business, Mr. Al Kiremli—in debt and with no startup capital—never stopped fighting for his dreams. He stepped immediately in the corporate sector, working as an employee in sales and business development in industries ranging from cladding materials, building materials, and heavy transportation to computer hardware and other key industries. Impressed and unfamiliar with the corporate business model (there had been no corporate environment in Iraq), Mr. Al Kiremli not only learned new skills, but also discovered the inherent problems in the corporate model. This realization prompted him to look for answers which led to the early development of his many methodologies in the areas of productivity and efficiency.

Within three years, having proven himself a successful manager of people and processes, his father and uncle asked Mr. Al Kiremli to take the helm as general manager of their 25 years old retail and wholesale stationary business—managing more than 50 employees. The same year, he launched his educational, training and consulting business (visit AhmedAlKiremli.com).

Two years later, at age 28, he launched the first-ever franchise restaurant in Iraq—a food-court restaurant concept called Iraqi Touch, with his mother as a silent partner for the first store of the chain. The first version failed due to a bad location, but the second restaurant—relocated into the leading shopping mall in Erbil, Iraq—was extremely successful until 2015, when the entry of ISIS forces into Iraq forced its closure. Today, it has been reconceived as a catering company serving the oil and gas exploration industry in southern Iraq.

Soon after launching Iraqi Touch, Mr. Al Kiremli followed with his second franchise—now the most successful video gaming franchise in the world: Games Corner, a gaming experience sited in shopping malls. Knowing that gamers wanted a unique gaming experience in a distinctive environment, Mr. Al Kiremli ignored the doubts of others who said gamers would never travel to a shopping mall when they could play the same games at home. The franchise has now grown to a dozen locations—including one in the world-leading mall (Dubai Mall)—with a goal of 1,000 locations worldwide over the next 20 years. Games Corner is the #1 mall-based gaming franchise worldwide.

Two other successful businesses followed: Climb and Slide, a soft-play brand for children—and Best Movie Ratings, an app that combines movie ratings from platforms like IMDB, Rotten Tomatoes, and Meta Critics with Mr. Al Kiremli's personal ratings to help moviegoers find the most impactful, uplifting and enriching movies to watch.

Mr. Al Kiremli was born and raised in Baghdad, the capital of Iraq—witnessing numerous wars, military attacks and their associated tragedies during his young life including the invasion of Kuwait; the Gulf War (which brought military forces from 30 different countries to his homeland); the Sha'aban Intifada in 1991; the Iraqi-Kurdish Civil War between 1995 and 1996; Operation Desert Fox in 1998; 2003 invasion of Iraq by a United States-led coalition, which toppled the government of Saddam Hussein; The Iraqi Civil War & other multiple conflicts between 2004 and until the current date; While those times were extremely difficult to live through (and even harder to conduct business), Mr. Al Kiremli learned priceless lessons that shaped the way he views the world and the way he appreciates life and success. He believes these experiences shaped his character and gave him the ability to handle pain and tragedy—developing in him not only long-term fortitude, but also strength of resolve in his business life.

Today, Mr. Al Kiremli lives and travels worldwide, operating his many business ventures while also playing in the Professional Squash Association (PSA)—competing against the finest players in the world and boosting his world Squash ranking in the process.

While every effort goes into ensuring that this book is flawless, it is inevitable that a mistake or two will slip through the cracks. If you find an error of any kind in this book, please let me know by visiting: www.ahmedalkiremli.com/typos

I appreciate you taking the time to notify me. This ensures that future readers never have to experience that awful typo. You are making the world a better place.

ACKNOWLEDGMENTS

No book is ever written—no entrepreneurial success is ever achieved—without the assistance and mentorship of many, many people. In my lifetime, I've been thankful to have had the guidance and wisdom of the following people who have helped me create the mindset, knowledge base and passion for success required to live a fulfilling life.

To my lovely wife, Irina, for being patient and supportive throughout the journey of writing this book.

To Adryan Russ, book editor extraordinaire. Without Adryan's superb developmental assistance and manuscript editing, my readers would not see this book in its current form.

To Patty Aubery, President of The Jack Canfield Companies, for introducing me to resources who could help me complete the manuscript and move forward with this book.

To Jack Canfield, America's #1 Success Coach, the beloved originator of the *Chicken Soup for the Soul®* book series, and a man who has launched 47 *New York Times* bestsellers—selling over 550 million books worldwide—I learned many things related to book structure, writing techniques, and book publishing.

To Robert Kiyosaki, author of numerous *New York Times* bestselling books including *Rich Dad, Poor Dad*—the #1 personal finance book of all time. Not only have I read over 15 of his books, I consider him my financial freedom mentor. I'm thankful for all the knowledge and wisdom I acquired from him and recommend all his books to anyone seeking to achieve financial freedom.

To all the outstanding guests of my web Tv show, *Be Efficient Tv.* Over the years, I've interviewed *New York Times* bestselling authors, founders of companies, CEOs, and experts from countless industries—

and I'm thankful to them for sharing the gift of their time, wisdom and knowledge with me and my viewers. Not only did their insights help me personally, they significantly impacted the writing, marketing, publishing and content of this book.

INDEX

Symbols

A

B

E

F

S

T